THE
ARISTOS

Books by John Fowles

THE COLLECTOR
THE ARISTOS
THE MAGUS
THE FRENCH LIEUTENANT'S WOMAN

THE
ARISTOS

by John Fowles

REVISED EDITION

Little, Brown and Company
Boston – Toronto

CONTENTS

PREFACE TO A NEW EDITION

THIS BOOK was first published against the advice of almost everyone who read it. I was told that it would do my 'image' no good; and I am sure that my belief that a favourable 'image' is conceivably not of any great human—or literary—significance would have counted for very little if I had not had a best-selling novel behind me. I used that 'success' to issue this 'failure', and so I face a charge of unscrupulous obstinacy. To the obstinacy I must plead guilty, but not to lack of scruple; for I was acting only in accordance with what I had written.

My chief concern, in *The Aristos,** is to preserve the freedom of the individual against all those pressures-to-conform that threaten our century; one of those pressures, put upon all of us, but particularly on anyone who comes into public notice, is that of labelling a person by what he gets money and fame for—by what other people most want to use him *as*. To call a man a plumber is to describe one aspect of him, but it is also to obscure a number of others. I am a writer; I want no more specific prison than that I express myself in printed words. So a prime personal reason for this book was to announce that I did not intend to walk into the cage labelled 'novelist'.

However, it was not just the matter of the book that offended. It was the manner as well—the dogmatic way in which I set out my views on life. But that too sprang from a desire to nourish individuality. By stating baldly what *I* believe I hope to force you to state baldly to yourself what *you* believe. I do not expect agreement. If I wanted that I should have written in a very different form and style,

---

* *aristos* is taken from the ancient Greek. It is singular and means roughly 'the best for a given situation'. It is stressed on the first syllable.

and wrapped my pills in the usual sugar coating. I am not, in short, *pleading* a case.

There is a very current view in our world that philosophy should be left to the philosophers, sociology to the sociologists, and death to the dead. I believe this is one of the great heresies—and tyrannies—of our time. I reject totally the view that in matters of general concern (such as the meaning of life, the nature of the good society, the limitations of the human condition) only the specialist has the right to have opinions—and then only in his own subject. *Trespassers will be prosecuted* signs have, thank goodness, become increasingly rare in our countryside; but they still spring like mushrooms round the high-walled estates of our literary and intellectual life. In spite of all our achievements in technology we are, outside our narrow professional fields, mentally one of the laziest and most sheep-like ages that has ever existed. Yet another purpose of this book is to suggest that the main reason dissatisfaction haunts our century, as optimism haunted the eighteenth and complacency the nineteenth, is precisely because we are losing sight of our most fundamental human birthright: to have a self-made opinion on all that concerns us.

By using the same method as Nelson for not reading unwanted signals, some critics have further seen in this book and in my two novels—*The Collector* and *The Magus*—evidence that I am a crypto-fascist. All my adult life I have believed that the only rational political doctrine one can hold is democratic socialism. But what I have never believed in is quasi-emotional liberalism of the kind that has become popular these last twenty years; the kind of view that goes more with avant-garde social milieu and fashionable newspapers than with any deep-held conviction or reasoned attempt to destroy reaction. Nor similarly have I much time for the theory that socialism is the sole property of the proletariat and that the chief voice in socialist policy must always be that of organized labour. We may owe the rise of socialism very considerably to the trade union movement; but it is time the umbilical cord was cut.

The principal theme in this book—as also in *The Collector*—has been similarly misunderstood. In essence it comes from a Greek philosopher, Heraclitus. We know very little of Heraclitus, since he lived before the great age of Greek philosophy, and all that remains of his work are a few pages of frequently obscure fragments. In a famous book—*The Open Society*—Professor Karl Popper has made a convincing case against Heraclitus (if for nothing else, because he influenced Plato) as the grandfather of modern totalitarianism. Now Heraclitus saw mankind divided into a moral and intellectual *élite* (the *aristoi,* the good ones, *not*—this is a later sense—the ones of noble birth) and an unthinking, conforming mass—*hoi polloi,* the many. Anyone can see how such a distinction plays into the hands of all those subsequent thinkers who have advanced theories of the master-race, the superman, government by the few or by the one, and the rest. One cannot deny that Heraclitus has, like some in itself innocent weapon left lying on the ground, been used by reactionaries: but it seems to me that his basic contention is *biologically* irrefutable.

In every field of human endeavour it is obvious that most of the achievements, most of the great steps forward have come from individuals—whether they be scientific or artistic geniuses, saints, revolutionaries, what you will. And we do not need the evidence of intelligence testing to know conversely that the vast mass of mankind are not highly intelligent—or highly moral, or highly gifted artistically, or indeed highly qualified to carry out any of the nobler human activities. Of course, to jump from that to the conclusion that mankind can be split into two clearly defined groups, a Few that is excellent and a Many that is despicable, is idiotic. The gradations are infinite; and if you carry no other idea away from this book I hope you will understand what I mean when I say that *the dividing line between the Few and the Many must run through each individual, not between individuals.* In short none of us are wholly perfect; and none wholly imperfect.

On the other hand, history—not least in the twentieth century—shows that society has persistently seen life in terms of a struggle between the Few and the Many, between 'Them' and 'Us'. My purpose in *The Collector* was to attempt to analyse, through a parable, some of the results of this confrontation. Clegg, the kidnapper, committed the evil; but I tried to show that his evil was largely, perhaps wholly, the result of a bad education, a mean environment, being orphaned: all factors over which he had no control. In short, I tried to establish the virtual *innocence* of the Many. Miranda, the girl he imprisoned, had very little more control than Clegg over what she was: she had well-to-do parents, good educational opportunity, inherited aptitude and intelligence. That does not mean that she was perfect. Far from it—she was arrogant in her ideas, a prig, a liberal-humanist snob, like so many university students. Yet if she had not died she might have become something better, the kind of being humanity so desperately needs.

The actual evil in Clegg overcame the potential good in Miranda. I did not mean by this that I view the future with a black pessimism; nor that a precious *élite* is threatened by the barbarian hordes. I meant simply that unless we face up to this unnecessarily brutal conflict (based largely on an unnecessary envy on the one hand and an unnecessary contempt on the other) between the biological Few and the biological Many; unless we admit that we are not, and never will be, born equal, though we are all born with equal human rights; unless the Many can be educated out of their false assumption of inferiority and the Few out of their equally false assumption that biological superiority is a state of existence instead of what it really is, *a state of responsibility*—then we shall never arrive at a more just and happier world.

Elsewhere in this book I maintain the importance of the

polar view of life; that individuals, nations, ideas are far more dependent for strength, energy and fuel on their opposites, enemies and contraries than surface appearances suggest. This is true too of the opposition between the Few and the Many, the evolutionally over- and under-privileged. There are healthy products, besides the obviously unhealthy ones, in this embattled condition. But if one word could sum up all that is wrong with our world, it is surely *inequality*. It was inequality, not Lee Harvey Oswald, that killed President Kennedy. Hazard, the great factor we shall never be able to control, will always infest life with inequality. And it seems madness that man himself should continue blindly to propagate this vicious virus in our world instead of trying to limit it.

This was the deeper message in *The Collector;* and in this present book. Whatever it may be it is not, I think you will agree, a fascist one.

This edition contains new material, but it is shorter (though not meant to be attempted at one sitting) than its predecessor and, I sincerely hope, much clearer. One other criticism of the first edition I fully deserved. There was an irritating swarm of new-coined words. These I have almost completely abolished.

1968

I should like to take advantage of this revised edition to say that I have, since this book was first written, become increasingly interested in its relevance to the American experience. There are two main reasons for this. The United States is the key society in our world—'key' both in the narrow sense of its being the guinea pig among human societies and in a broader one: the country where the struggle between individual freedom and social equality is being conducted (largely because of an innate national honesty) at its most naked and revealing. The second reason is an ever-deepening affection and respect for the better qualities of the American ethos combined, alas, with an ever-deepening distress at its less happy effects.

I hope shortly to finish what will constitute a kind of appendix to *The Aristos:* a sympathetic critique, in the light of some of the ideas here, of the country that has for so long held so many of us Europeans in its complex spell.

1970

INTRODUCTION

1 The book you are about to begin is written in the form of notes. This is not laziness on my part, but an attempt to suppress all rhetoric, all persuasion through style. Many of the notes are dogmatic expressions of opinion; and here, similarly, my intention is not to bludgeon into belief, but to banish all possibility of persuasion by artificial means. I do not want my ideas to be liked merely because they are likeably presented; I want them to be liked in themselves.

2 This is not a dialogue, but only one side of a dialogue. I state; you, if you wish, refute.

3 Some of what I say suffers from the usual defect of speculation and generalization; there is no proof. What proof there is lies in your agreement; what disproof, in your disagreement. Many modern philosophers would claim that unverifiable statements are scientifically meaningless; but I cannot agree that philosophy is, or will ever be, only a science.*

4 I am a poet first; and then a scientist. That is a biographical fact, not a recommendation.

5 I believe in the essential sanity of man, and what follows is a memorial to that belief.

* An asterisk indicates a note at the end of this book.

1

THE UNIVERSAL SITUATION

1 Where are we? What is this situation? Has it a master?

2 Matter in time appears to us, with our vested interest in survival, to be governed by two opposing principles: Law, or the organizing principle, and Chaos, or the disintegrating one. These two, the one to us sorting and erecting, the other to us demolishing and causing havoc, are in eternal conflict. This conflict is existence.

3 All that exists has, by existing and by not being the only thing that exists, individuality.

4 The known universe is uniform in its constituents and its laws. All in it, or each individual thing, has a birth and a death in time. This birth and this death are the insignia of individuality.

5 The forms of matter are finite, but matter is infinite. Form is a death sentence, matter is eternal life.

6 Individuality is necessary for both the sensation of pain and the feeling of pleasure. Pains and pleasures both serve the one end of the whole: survival of matter. All pains and pleasures are partly what they are because they are not shared; and because, being functions of an individual, they end.

7 Law and Chaos, the two processes that dominate ex-

istence, are equally indifferent to the individual. To Chaos, Law destroys; to Law, Chaos. They equally create, dictate to and destroy the individual.

8 In the whole, nothing is unjust. It may, to this or that individual, be unfortunate.

9 There can be no power or god in the whole that is concerned for any one thing, though there may be a power concerned for the whole.

10 The whole has no favourites.

THE WRECK AND THE RAFT

11 Humanity on its raft. The raft on the endless ocean. From his present dissatisfaction man reasons that there was some catastrophic wreck in the past, before which he was happy; some golden age, some Garden of Eden. He also reasons that somewhere ahead lies a promised land, a land without conflict. Meanwhile, he is miserably *en passage;* this myth lies deeper than religious faith.

12 Seven men inhabit the raft. The pessimist, for whom the good things of life are no more than lures to prolong suffering; the egocentric, whose motto is *Carpe diem*—enjoy today—and who does his best to get the most comfortable part of the raft for himself; the optimist, always scanning the horizon for the promised land; the observer, who finds it enough to write the logbook of the voyage and to note down the behaviour of the sea, the raft and his fellow-victims; the altruist, who finds his reason for being in the need to deny himself and to help others; the stoic, who believes in nothing but his own refusal to jump over-

board and end it all; and finally the child, the one born, as some with perfect pitch, with perfect ignorance—the pitifully ubiquitous child, who believes that all will be explained in the end, the nightmare fade and the green shore rise.

13   But there was no wreck; there will be no promised land. If there ever were an ideal promised land, a Canaan, it would be uninhabitable to humans.

14   Man is a seeker of the agent. We seek an agent for this being in a blind wind, this being on a raft; the mysterious power, the causator, the god, the face behind the mysterious mask of being and not being. Some make an active god of their own better natures; a benevolent father, a gentle mother, a wise brother, a charming sister. Some make an active god from attributes: such desirable human attributes as mercy, concern and justice. Some make an active god of their own worse natures; a god who is sadistically cruel or profoundly absurd; a god who absconds; a black exploiter of the defenceless individual; the venomous tyrant of *Genesis 3:16–17*.

15   Between these tribes, the firm believers in an active good god and the firm believers in an active bad one, the great majority shift and surge, a milling herd caught between Pangloss and Job. They pay lip service to an empty image; or believe in nothing. In this century they have drifted towards Job. If there is an active good god he has, since 1914, paid very poor wages.*

16   Yet as man sees through one reason for living, another wells from the mysterious spring. It must be so, because he continues to exist. This inexplicable buoyancy irritates him. He exists, but he is abused.

17 Man is an everlack, an infinite withoutness, afloat on an apparently endless ocean of apparently endless indifference to individual things. Obscurely he sees catastrophes happening to other rafts, rafts that are too distant for him to determine whether they have other humans aboard, but too numerous and too identical for him to presume that they have not.

18 He lives in a survived yet always uncertainly surviving world. All that is has survived where it might not have survived. Every world is and will always be a Noah's ark.

19 The old myth that his raft, his world, is especially favoured and protected now seems ridiculous. He has seen and understood the message from the distant supernovae; he knows the sun is growing larger and hotter and that his world will one day be a white-hot ball in a sea of flames; and he knows that the hydrogen bomb of the sun may burn up an already dead planet. There are other hydrogen bombs waiting and closer at hand. Inwards and outwards the prospect before him is terrifying.*

THE NECESSITY OF HAZARD

20 But mankind is in the best of all possible situations *for mankind*. It may not be the best possible for you or for me, for this or that individual; for this or that age; for this or that world.

21 It is the best possible for us because it is an infinite situation of finite hazard: that is, its fundamental principle will always be hazard, but a hazard within bounds. A hazard without bounds would be a universe without physical laws: that is, a perpetual and total chaos.

22 A god who revealed his will, who 'heard' us, who answered our prayers, who was propitiable, the kind of god simple people like to imagine would be desirable: such a god would destroy all our hazard, all our purpose and all our happiness.

23 Hazard has conditioned us to live in hazard. All our pleasures are dependent on it. Even though I arrange for a pleasure, and look forward to it, my eventual enjoyment of it is still a matter of hazard. Wherever time passes, there is hazard. You may die before you turn the next page.

24 I am is I was not, I might not have been, I may not be, I shall not be.

25 In order that we should have meaning, purpose and pleasure it has been, is, and always will be necessary that we live in a whole that is indifferent to every individual thing in it; and the precise form of its indifference is that the duration of being and the fortune during being of each individual thing are fundamentally but not unconditionally in hazard.

26 What we call suffering, death, disaster, misfortune, tragedy, we should call the price of freedom. The only alternative to this suffering freedom is an unsuffering unfreedom.

THE GODGAME

27 Imagine yourself a god, and lay down the laws of a universe. You then find yourself in the Divine Predicament: good governors must govern all equally, and all fairly. But no act of government can be fair to all, in all their different situations, except one.

28 The Divine Solution is to govern by not governing in any sense that the governed can call being governed; that is, to constitute a situation in which the governed must govern themselves.

29 If there had been a creator, his second act would have been to disappear.

30 Put dice on the table and leave the room; but make it seem possible to the players that you were never in the room.

31 The good human and so the good universal upbringing gives freedom to develop, or hazard, within fixed bounds.

32 The whole is not a pharaonic cosmos; a blind obsession with pyramids, assembling, slaves. Our pyramid has no apex; it is not a pyramid. We are not slaves who will never see the summit, because there *is* no summit. Life may be less imperfect in a hundred years' time than it is today; but it will be even less imperfect a hundred years after that. Perfectibility is meaningless because wherever we enter the infinite *processus* we can look forward with a kind of nostalgia for the future, and imagine a better age. It is also evil, because a terminus of perfection breeds a cancer of now. For perfectibilitarians, perfect ends tomorrow justify very imperfect means today.

33 We build towards nothing; we build.

34 Our universe is the best possible because it can contain no Promised Land; no point where we could have all we imagine. We are designed to want: with nothing to want, we are like windmills in a world without wind.

35   Emily Dickinson: *If summer were an axiom, what sorcery had snow?**

36   We are in the best possible situation because everywhere, below the surface, we do not know; we shall never know why; we shall never know tomorrow; we shall never know a god or if there is a god; we shall never even know ourselves. This mysterious wall round our world and our perception of it is not there to frustrate us but to train us back to the now, to life, to our time being.

FINITY AND INFINITY

37   The cosmos is an infinite proliferation of fire, atoms, forms, collisions, attractions, sports, mutations, all happening in the space-time continuum; only thus can Law survive against Chaos, and only thus can Chaos survive against Law.

38   Only in an infinitely proliferating cosmos can both order and disorder coexist infinitely; and the only purposeful cosmos must be one that proliferates infinitely. It was therefore not created, but was always.

39   A finite creation is incomprehensible. If a creator were not self-sufficient, it would be absurd to suppose that there was both a time when he was aware of this and did nothing, and a time when he remedied his deficiency. What is easier to believe? That there was always something or that there was once nothing?

40   Christianity says that creation has a beginning, middle and end. The Greeks claimed that creation is a timeless *processus*. Both are correct. All that is created

and is therefore individual has a beginning and an
end; but there is no universal beginning and end.

41 Our universe may fall in on itself, the red shift change
to a blue. All universes may be like an expanding and
contracting heart, with the spores of humanity growing in the cool spaces between stars; then withering in
the autumn collapse. Or they may expand eternally.

42 A phoenix infinity; or an infinite expansion. Whichever it is, the astrophysicists now know what Hora-
clitus guessed: that suns must grow in heat and finally
consume their planetary systems. Look out of the
window: everything you see is frozen fire in transit
between fire and fire. Cities, equations, lovers, landscapes: all are hurtling towards the hydrogen crucible.*

43 Even if we could establish a definite point of genesis
for our own universe, we could never establish the
genesis of what may or may not lie beyond the limits
of our observational power. It is convenient to behave
in science as if what may lie beyond our present
domain of knowledge does not exist; but the logical
chances are even, and the practical probabilities all on
my side.

44 Nothing is unique in its species, even a cosmos;
though everything is unique in its own existing.

45 If a cosmos is infinite, it has no end. If it has no end,
there can be no end it is serving. Its only end must lie
in its means. It exists in order to exist.

46 Only one process allows all conscious beings to have
equal importance: an infinite one. If there were any

end to which evolution was tending, then you and I would be slaves of a pharaoh, a builder of pyramids. But if there is no end, and only in an infinite universe can there be no end, then you, from whatever world or age you come, and I are equal. For both of us the slope is the same, and reaches as far ahead and as far behind. This is the great proof that the whole is infinite. *It was never created and it will never end, so that all that is may be equal in it.*

'GOD'

47 I put the word in inverted commas in order to except it from its common meanings; to purge it of all its human associations.

48 'God' is a situation. Not a power, or a being, or an influence. Not a 'he' or a 'she', but an 'it'. Not entity or non-entity, but the situation in which there can be both entity and non-entity.

49 Because people cannot understand that what is not can influence what is, they maintain that 'God' is and does. But our ignorance of 'God' and its motives will always remain infinite. To ask *What is God?* is as futile as to ask *When does infinity begin and end?*

50 Existence is ultimately or potentially knowable; 'God' is infinitely unknowable. The most we shall ever learn is why existence is *as it is;* why it requires such laws and such constituents to continue. We shall never learn ultimately *why* it is.

51 St Augustine: *We know only what God is not.* Existence is individual, therefore 'God' is not individual. Existence changes, therefore 'God' does not. Exist-

ence has power to intervene, therefore 'God' does not. Existence is finite, therefore 'God' is not. But 'God' is omnipresent, since all that exists (and is therefore individual) is not.*

52 'God' is not; but its not-being is universally present, and universally affects. It cannot exist in any sense meaningful to material organisms; but that does not mean that this situation is meaningless to such organisms. If, for instance, you see two men fighting, but do not intervene (although you could have intervened), then in fact you intervene by not intervening; and it is so with 'God'.

53 The whole is intrinsically a situation in which the principles and the events are all, and the individual thing is nothing. Since it is thus completely indifferent to the individual thing, 'God' must be totally sympathetic to the whole. But it expresses its sympathy by not being and by its total unknowability. It is *wu wei* and *wu ming,* without action and without name.

54 *Tao Te Ching:*
    LXVII. If it resembled anything it would long before now have become insignificant.
    LVII. The sage says, I do nothing and the people change of themselves. I prefer stillness and the people correct themselves. I do not intervene and the people prosper by themselves.
    LI. It gives the myriads life and yet claims no possession; it benefits them yet asks for no thanks; it looks after them yet exercises no authority.
    *X. Can you love the people and govern the state without resorting to action?**

55 If the individual thing suffers, it is so that the whole may not. This can happen only in a world of indi-

vidualized matter, in which hazard, time and change
are fundamental features.

THE CONTINGENCY OF MATTER

56 The concept of infinity bans any purpose except that
    of infinity. If we experience sensations of happiness,
    then it must be because matter in the form of human
    beings experiencing happiness serves the purpose of
    infinity, which is the maintenance of infinity. For to
    be happy to exist is to want to continue to exist.

57 But if the purpose of the whole is simply to prolong
    itself, what is the necessity of evolution, of causation,
    of complex physical laws? Why introduce the expe-
    rience of pleasure, let alone the consciousness of
    pleasure? Why could not existence be an eternal stone
    in an eternal vacuum, or an infinite cloud of static
    atoms? To man the answer has always seemed simple.
    The gods wish their handiwork to be admired; they
    want libation, psalm and sacrifice. But this is the old
    and pernicious heresy of the anthropocentric universe,
    in which we humans are the Few and all the lower
    rest of creation, the Many. In such a universe we must
    assume a very active god; and one who is very much
    on our side, a suspiciously prejudiced figure to be in
    command of the whole.

58 Then why should matter exist at all? A single hydro-
    gen atom must seem, if the sole purpose of infinity is
    infinity, a redundancy. But infinity cannot be of time
    alone. Time in itself, absolutely, does not exist; it is
    always relative to some observer or some object.
    Without a clock I say 'I do not know the time'.
    Without matter, time itself is unknowable; and infinity
    does not exist.

59 Time is a function of matter; and matter therefore is the clock that makes infinity real. From our very special human standpoint some changes in the form of matter—such as the leap in anthropoid brain size, the appearance of self-consciousness, the discovery of tools, of language—are unmistakable evidence of some beneficent universal intention towards us. But all this might appear, to some hypothetical outside observer, a mere result of the effects of time on matter. He would not see it in terms of *progress*—the present complexity of matter might indeed seem to be a regress, a devolution, a superfluous ornamentation —but in terms of *process*.

60 To this outside observer all the special privileges we claim for our species, all the feathers in our cap, might seem as absurd as the exotic ceremonial finery of some primitive chieftain; of no more significance than the flowers in my garden for a surveyor. My flowers may mean a great deal to me; but I cannot assume that the purpose of evolution is to give them to me.

61 What we call evolutionary progress is so for nothing but ourselves. The very term 'evolution', with its assumption of development-from, is misleading. We are like the observer in sub-atomic physics who distorts the nature of the particle observed by the very act of observation.

62 This indifference of the process to the individual objects that constitute it, this 'God' which is a situation and not a person, which does not intervene, this blind obsession with the maintenance of infinity—all this may appear to leave our human world intolerably bare. But even here one can detect evidence of a universal sympathy. How can we not see? By not being

in our sense of being, by not intervening, 'God' is a warning to us that *Homo sapiens,* like every other form of matter, is not necessary, but contingent. If our world is annihilated, and all of us with it, the whole will not suffer. It is madness, a delusion we inherit from our remotest ancestors, to suppose that thanksgiving can influence the course of events; that these man-like projections of our own wishful thinking can intervene on our behalf in the process.*

63 No one will save us but ourselves; and the final proof of the sympathy in 'God' lies in the fact that we are— or can by exercise become—free to choose courses of action and so at least combat some of the hostile results of the general indifference of the process to the individual.

64 Freedom of will is the highest human good; and it is impossible to have both that freedom and an intervening divinity. We, because we are a form of matter, are contingent; and this terrifying contingency allows our freedom.

MYSTERY

65 We shall never know finally why we are; why anything is, or needs to be. All our science, all our art, the whole vast edifice of matter, has its foundations in this meaninglessness; and the only assumptions we can make about it are that it is both necessary and sympathetic to the continuing existence of matter.

66 We want to be mastered, but we are masterless. We think always in a causative and hierarchical manner. The process and 'God' are co-infinite. Our finity cannot comprehend them, or their causelessness.

67 'God' is caused by what it causes; is made necessary by what it necessitates; we cannot comprehend.

68 We go on living, in the final analysis, because we do not know why we are here to live. Unknowing, or hazard, is as vital to man as water.

69 We can imagine the non-existence of any existent object. Our belief that it does exist is partly assured by the fact that it might not have done so. Behind the shape, the mass, there stands always the absence; the ghost of non-existing.

70 Just as the atom is made of positive and negative particles, so is each thing made of its own existence and non-existence. Thus is 'God' present by being absent in every thing and every moment. It is the dark core, the mystery, the being-not-being of even the simplest objects.

71 Erigena: *God is eternally partially self-ignorant. If he know all of himself, he could define himself. If he could define himself, he would be finite. But all he knows of himself is what he has created. What is created is his knowledge, what is potential is his mystery: mysterious in him and to him.**

   All this applies equally to man.

72 The ubiquitous absence of 'God' in ordinary life is this sense of non-existing, of mystery, of incalculable potentiality; this eternal doubt that hovers between the thing in itself and our perception of it; this dimension in and by which all other dimensions exist. The white paper that contains a drawing; the space that contains a building; the silence that contains a sonata; the passage of time that prevents a sensation or object continuing for ever; all these are 'God'.

73 Mystery, or unknowing, is energy. As soon as a mystery is explained, it ceases to be a source of energy. If we question deep enough there comes a point where answers, if answers could be given, would kill. We may want to dam the river; but we dam the spring at our peril. In fact, since 'God' is unknowable, we cannot dam the spring of basic existential mystery. 'God' is the energy of all questions and questing; and so the ultimate source of all action and volition.

ATHEISM

74 I do not consider myself an atheist, yet this concept of 'God' and our necessary masterlessness obliges me to behave in all public matters as if I were.

75 Whatever sympathy I feel towards religions, whatever admiration for some of their adherents, whatever historical or biological necessity I see in them, whatever metaphorical truth, I cannot accept them as credible explanations of reality; and they are incredible to me in proportion to the degree that they require my belief in positive human attributes and intervenient powers in their divinities.

76 I live in hazard and infinity. The cosmos stretches around me, meadow on meadow of galaxies, reach on reach of dark space, steppes of stars, oceanic darkness and light. There is no amenable god in it, no particular concern or particular mercy. Yet everywhere I see a living balance, a rippling tension, an enormous yet mysterious simplicity, an endless breathing of light. And I comprehend that being is understanding that I must exist in hazard but that the whole is not in hazard. Seeing and knowing this is being conscious; accepting it is being human.

2

HUMAN DISSATISFACTIONS

1 Why do we think this is not the best of all possible worlds for mankind? Why are we unhappy in it?

2 What follow are the great dissatisfactions. I maintain that they are all essential to our happiness since they provide the soil from which it grows.

DEATH

3 We hate death for two reasons. It ends life prematurely; and we do not know what lies beyond it.

4 A very large majority of educated mankind now doubts the existence of an afterlife. It is clear that the only scientific attitude is that of agnosticism: we simply do not know. We are in the Bet Situation.*

5 The Bet Situation is one in which we cannot have certainty about some future event; and yet in which it is vital that we come to a decision about its nature. This situation faces us at the beginning of a horse race, when we want to know the name of the winner. We are reduced at worst to guessing it with a pin and at best to forecasting it intelligently from the evidence of past form, condition in the paddock, and all the rest. Most serious gamblers know that their interest is better served by the second method; and it is this method we should use when we come to wager on the race between an afterlife and a total extinction. We

have two horses, but of course three choices, since we can argue that it is best not to bet—that is, to remain agnostic.

6 To Pascal, who first made this analogy with the bet, the answer was clear: one must put one's money on the Christian belief that a recompensatory afterlife exists. If it is not true, he argued, then one has lost nothing but one's stake. If it is true, one has gained all.

7 Now even an atheist contemporary with Pascal might have agreed that nothing but good could ensue, in an unjust society where the majority conveniently believed in hellfire, from supporting the idea, false or true, of an afterlife. But today the concept of hellfire has been discarded by the theologians, let alone the rest of us. Hell could be just only in a world where all were equally persuaded that it exists; just only in a world that allowed a total freedom of will—and therefore a total biographical and biological similarity —to every man and woman in it. We may still disagree on the extent to which man is determined in his behaviour by exterior circumstances, but that he is not partly so determined is irrefutable.

8 The idea of an afterlife has persistently haunted man because inequality has persistently tyrannized him. It is not only to the poor, the sick, the unfortunate underdogs of history, that the idea appeals; it has appealed to all honest men's sense of justice, and very often at the same time as the use of the idea to maintain an unequal *status quo* in society has revolted them. Somewhere, this belief proposes, there is a system of absolute justice and a day of absolute judgement, by and on which we are all to be rewarded according to our deserts.

9   But the true longing of humanity is not for an after-
    life; it is for the establishment of a justice here and
    now that will make an afterlife unnecessary. This
    myth was a compensatory fantasy, a psychological
    safety-valve for the frustrations of existential reality.

10 We are ourselves to establish justice in our world; and
    the more we allow the belief in an afterlife to dwindle
    away, and yet still do so little to correct the flagrant
    inequalities of our world, then the more danger we
    run.

11 Our world has a badly-designed engine. By using the
    oil of this myth it did not for many centuries heat up.
    But now the oil-level is dropping ominously low. For
    this reason, it is not enough to remain agnostic. We
    must bet on the other horse: we have one life, and it
    is ended by a total extinction of consciousness as well
    as body.

12 What matters is not our personal damnation or salva-
    tion in the world to come, but that of our fellow men
    in the world that is.

13 Our second hatred of death is that it almost always
    comes too soon. We suffer from an illusion, akin to
    that of the desirability of an afterlife, that we should
    be happier if we lived for ever. Animal desires are
    always for an extension of what satisfies them. Only
    two hundred years ago a man who reached the age
    of forty was exceeding the average life-span; and
    perhaps two hundred years from now centenarians
    will be as common as septuagenarians today. But
    they will still crave a longer life.

14 The function of death is to put tension into life; and
    the more we increase the length and the security of

individual existence then the more tension we remove from it. All our pleasurable experiences contain a faint yet terrible element of the condemned man's last breakfast, an echo of the intensity of feeling of the poet who knows he is going to die, of the young soldier going doomed into battle.

15   Each pleasure we feel is a pleasure less; each day a stroke on a calendar. What we will not accept is that the joy in the day and the passing of the day are inseparable. What makes our existence worthwhile is precisely that its worth and its while—its quality and duration—are as impossible to unravel as time and space in the mathematics of relativity.

16   *Pleasure is a product of death; not an escape from it.*

17   If it were proved that there is an afterlife, life would be irretrievably spoilt. It would be pointless; and suicide, a virtue. *The only possible paradise is one in which I cannot know I did once exist.*

18   There are two tendencies in the twentieth century; one, a misguided one, is to domesticate death, to pretend that death is like life; the other is to look death in the face. The tamers of death believe in life after death; they indulge in elaborate after-death ceremonial. Their attitude to death is euphemistic; it is 'passing on' and 'going to a better place'. The actual process of death and decomposition is censored. Such people are in the same mental condition as the ancient Egyptians.

19   'Passing on': the visual false analogy. We know that passing objects, such as we see repeatedly every day, exist both before and after the passage that we see;

and so we come, illogically and wrongly, to treat life
as such a passage.

20 Death is in us and outside us; beside us in every room,
in every street, in every field, in every car, in every
plane. Death is what we are not every moment that
we are, and every moment that we are is the moment
when the dice comes to rest. We are always playing
Russian roulette.

21 Being dead is nothingness, not-being. When we die
we constitute 'God'. Our relics, our monuments, the
memories retained by those who survive us, these still
exist; do not constitute 'God', still constitute the process. But these relics are the fossilized traces of our
having been, not our being. All the great religions try
to make out that death is nothing. There is another
life to come. But why only for humans? Or why only
for humans and animals? Why not for inanimate
things? When did it begin for humans? Before Peking
man, or after?

22 As one social current has tried to hide death, to
euphemize it out of existence, so another has thrust
death forward as a chief element in entertainment:
in the murder story, the war story, the spy story,
the western. But increasingly, as our century grows
old, these fictive deaths become more fictitious, and
fulfil the function of concealed euphemism. The real
death of a pet kitten affects a child far more deeply
than the 'deaths' of all the television gangsters, cow-
boys and Red Indians.

23 By death we think characteristically of the disappearance of individuals; it does not console us to know
that matter is not disappearing, but is simply being

metamorphosed. We mourn the individualizing form, not the generalized content. But everything we see is a metaphor of death. Every limit, every dimension, every end of every road, is a death. Even seeing is a death, for there is a point beyond which we cannot see, and our seeing dies; wherever our capacity ends, we die.

24   Time is the flesh and blood of death; death is not a skull, a skeleton, but a clock face, a sun hurtling through a sea of thin gas. A part of you has died since you began to read this sentence.

25   Death itself dies. Every moment you live, it dies. *O Death where is thy sting, Death I will be thy death.* The living prove this; not the dead.

26   In all the countries living above a bare subsistence level, the twentieth century has seen a sharp increase in awareness of the pleasures of life. This is not only because of the end of belief in an afterlife, but because death is more real today, more probable, now that the H-bomb is.

27   *The more absolute death seems, the more authentic life becomes.*

28   All I love and know may be burnt to ashes in one small hour: London, New York, Paris, Athens gone in less time than it takes to count ten. I was born in 1926; and because of what can happen now in ten seconds, that year lies not forty-one years but a measureless epoch and innocence away. Yet I do not regret that innocence. I love life more, not less.

29   Death contains me as my skin contains me. Without

it, I am not what I am. Death is not a sinister door I
walk towards; it is my walking towards.

30 Because I am a man death is my wife; and now she
has stripped, she is beautiful, she wants me to strip,
to be her mate. This is necessity, this is love, this is
being-for-another, nothing else. I cannot escape this
situation, nor do I want to. She wants me to make
love, not like some man-eating spider, to consume
me, but like a wife in love, so that we can celebrate
our total sympathy, be fertile and bear children. It is
her effect on me and my effect upon her that make all
that is good in my time being. She is not a prostitute
or a mistress I am ashamed of or want to forget or
about whom I can sometimes pretend that she does
not exist. Like my real wife she informs every important situation in my life, she is wholly *of* my life, not
beyond, or against, or opposite to it. I accept her completely, in every sense of the word, and I love and
respect her for what she is to me.

HAVING ONLY THIS

31 One consequence of our new awareness of death must
be, and has been, an alarming growth of both national
and individual selfishness, a Gadarene rush to enjoy
the pleasures of the shops and senses before they close
for ever. History will no doubt decide that such a rush
was indeed the most striking event of the third quar-
ter of our century; for it has not been the economic
conditions that have fostered the current desire to
spend and enjoy regardless of the historical situation,
but ever more nakedly seen death that has created the
tomorrow-we-die economic conditions.

32 Such terms as 'affluent society' and 'conspicuous
consumption' are euphemisms, in the context of our

poverty-stricken and starvation-ridden world, for
selfishness.

33 I was taught to swim by an instructor of the old
school. He gave us two lessons. In the first we were
allowed lifejackets and he showed us the movements
of the breast-stroke; in the second he took away the
jackets and pushed us into the deep end of the pool.
That is where man is now. His first instinct is to turn
back to the rail and cling to it; but somehow he has to
force himself out and swim.

34 Eventual non-being is our common ground. Once
humanity realizes this any but the most nearly just
world becomes insufficient. To try, as some religions
and political creeds still do, to persuade people that
what happens in this world is fundamentally unimportant, since its injustices will all be corrected in the
next—in the shape of an afterlife or some political
Utopia—is to be on the devil's side. And tacitly to
support this belief by remaining agnostic is little
better.

35 The driver of a truck carrying high explosives drives
more carefully than the driver of one loaded with
bricks; and the driver of a high-explosives truck who
does not believe in a life after death drives more carefully than one who does.

36 Convince a man that he has only this life and he will
do what most of us do about the houses we live in.
They may not be the most desirable houses we can
imagine, we may wish they were larger, more beautiful, newer, older—but we accept that this is the
house we have to live in now, and we do our best to
make it habitable. I am not a temporary tenant, a
casual lodger in my present life. It is my house, and
the only one I shall ever own. *I have only this.*

THE MYTH OF A SOUL

37 When I was a child my Cornish grandmother told me that the pure white husks of cuttlefish I sometimes found in the jetsam along the shore were the souls of drowned sailors; and some such concrete image as this of countless centuries of folk-belief has remained in all of us, even though intellectually we know what I discovered about the cuttle-bones: that eventually they go yellow and crumble into dust.

38 Man has had to accept that his body cannot survive death. So he takes the most inaccessible and mysterious part of it, the brain, and claims that some of its functionings survive death.

39 There is no thought, no perception, no consciousness of it, no consciousness of consciousness, that cannot be traced to an electrochemical event in the brain. 'I have an immortal and immaterial soul' is a thought or statement; it is also a recording of the activity of certain cells by other cells.

40 A machine as complex as the human brain would also develop a self-consciousness, a conscience, and a 'soul'. It would take pleasure in being the complex machine it was; it would grow metaphysical myths about itself. All that is is constructible and therefore destructible: not magic; not 'super-natural'; not 'psychic'.

41 Machines are made from 'dead' matter; brains are made from 'living' matter. But the frontier between 'dead' and 'living' is confused. One could not construct a machine as complex as the brain out of 'dead'

matter; but part of the complexity (as proved by its actual inconstructibility) of the brain is that its machinery is made of 'living' matter. Our inability to construct mechanical yet fully human brains shows our scientific and technological inadequacy, not any real difference of category between the machine and the brain; between mechanical functions and supposedly 'spiritual' thoughts.

42   What survives death is putrescent stopped machinery. The consciousness is a mirror reflecting a mirror reflecting a mirror; anything that enters this room can be endlessly reflected and its reflections reflected. But when the room is demolished, no mirrors, no reflections; nothing.

43   The myth of a separate consciousness partly arises because of the loose way we use 'I'. 'I' becomes an object—a third thing. We are constantly in situations where we feel ourselves inadequate and where we think either 'It is not my fault, since I am not the person I would have chosen to be' or 'It is my fault'. These self-criticisms and excuses give us an illusion of objectivity, of being able to judge ourselves. We therefore devise a thing that judges, a separate 'soul'. But this 'soul' is no more than the ability to observe, to remember and to compare, and to create and to store ideals of conduct. This is mechanism, not ectoplasm; the human brain, not the Holy Ghost.

44   Life is the price we pay for death, not the reverse. The worse our life, the more we pay; the better, the cheaper. Evolution is the growth of experience, of intelligence, of knowledge, and this growth engenders moments of insight, moments when we see deeper purposes, truer causes, more intended effects. We stand at this great insight now: there is no life after

death. Soon this will be as certain to everyone as it is certain to me, where I write, that there is no one in the next room. It is true that I cannot absolutely prove there is no one without going into the room; but *all* the circumstantial evidence supports my belief. Death is the room that is always empty.

45 The great linked myths of the afterlife and the immortal soul have served their purpose; have stood between us and reality. But their going will change all, and is meant to change all.

ISOLATION

46 The old religions and philosophies were refuges, kind to man in a world that his ignorance of science and technology made unkind. Never try to pass us by, they always said, for behind us is nothing but misery and horror.

47 It is cold and bare outside, says the mother; but one day the child goes out. This age is still our first day out, and we feel ourselves alone; more free and more alone.

48 Our stereotyping societies force us to feel more alone. They stamp masks on us and isolate out real selves. We all live in two worlds: the old comfortable man-centred world of absolutes and the harsh real world of relatives. The latter, the relativity reality, terrifies us; and isolates and dwarfs us all.

49 Greater social concern may, paradoxically, only increase this isolation. The more society interferes and supervises and plays the good Samaritan, the less needed and lonelier the secret individual gets.

50 More and more we know how far we are from the persons we should like to be. Less and less do we believe that a man can be any other than he is born and conditioned to be. The more science reveals our mechanical nature the more a harried 'free' man, a Robin Hood in each, retreats into the forests of the private mind.

51 Yet all these lonelinesses are a part of our growing up, of our first going out alone, of our freedom. A child is protected from such fear and loneliness by having a falsely kind and simple mirage erected around him. He grows up and goes out into loneliness and reality and there he builds a more real protection against his isolation out of love and friendship and feeling for his fellow men.

52 Once again the indifferent process of infinity seems at first sight to have trapped us into a corner. But we are trapped only by our own stupidity and weakness. The escape is clear.

THE ANXIETIES

53 Anxiety is the name we give to an unpleasant effect on us, and personal to us, of the general necessity for hazard. All anxieties are in some sense goads. They may goad the weak beyond endurance; but it is essential that humanity as a whole is goaded.

54 In a happy world all anxieties would be games. An anxiety is a lack that causes pain; a game is a lack that causes pleasure. Two different men in identical circumstances: what one may feel is an anxiety, while to the other it is a game.

55 Anxieties are tensions between a pole in our real life and a counterpole in the life we imagine we would like to lead.

56 There are esoteric metaphysical anxieties and practical daily anxieties. There are fundamental universal anxieties and special individual anxieties. The more sensitive and self-conscious and aware of others man becomes, the more anxious, in his present ill-organized world, he is going to become.

57 Anxieties:
    The anxiety of the ignorance of the meaning of life.
    The anxiety of not knowing the future.
    The anxiety of death.
    The anxiety of choosing right. Where will my choices lead? Can I choose?
    The anxiety of otherness. All is other to me, including most of myself.
    The anxiety of responsibility.
    The anxiety of inability to love and help others: our family, our friends, our country, all men. This is aggravated by our increased other-awareness.
    The anxiety of not being loved by others.
    The anxieties of the *respublica*—social injustice, the H-bomb, starvation, racialism, brink policies, chauvinism, and the rest.
    The anxiety of ambition. Am I the person I want to be? Am I the person others (my employers, my family, my friends) want me to be?
    The anxieties of social position. Of class, of birth, of money, of status in society.
    The anxiety of money. Have I the necessities of life? There are situations in which a private yacht and a gallery of old masters may seem necessities of life.
    The anxiety of time. Have I the time to do what I want?

The anxiety of sex.

The anxiety of work. Am I doing the right work? Am I doing it as well as it needs to be done?

The anxiety of health.

58 To be alone in an office—dozens of telephones all ringing at the same time. These anxieties should make us one. We all feel them. But we let them isolate us, as if the citizens of a country would defend it by each barricading himself in his own house.

HAZARD

59 My only certainty in life is that I shall one day die. I can be certain of nothing else in the future. But either we survive (and so far in human history a vast majority has always survived) and having survived when we might not have done so gives us what we call happiness; or we do not survive and do not know it.

60 Hazard is essential for an evolutionary process. Some personal effects of it make us unhappy, because hazard is by definition inegalitarian. It is indifferent to law and to justice, as we understand those terms.

61 The purpose of hazard is to force us, and the rest of matter, to evolve. It is only by evolving that we, in a process that is evolving, can continue to survive. The purpose of *human* evolution is therefore to recognize this: that we must evolve to exist. And that we should extirpate unnecessary inequality—in other words, limit hazard in the human sphere—is an obvious corollary. There is therefore no more sense in being

unhappy at hazard in general than there is in hating
hands because they can be cut off; or in not taking
every precaution to see that they shall not be cut off.

ENVY

62 Our knowledge of what the richer than ourselves
    possess, and the poorer do not, has never been more
    widespread. Therefore envy, which is wanting what
    others have, and jealousy, which is not wanting others
    to have what one has, have also never been more
    widespread.

63 Each age has its mythical happy man: the one with
    wisdom, with genius, with saintliness, with beauty,
    with whatever is rare and the Many are not able
    to possess. The twentieth century's happy man is the
    man with money. Since our belief in a rewarding
    afterlife has decayed more quickly than our capacity
    to create a rewarding present life has grown, there
    was never a fiercer determination touch the paragon.

64 We are born with cleverness, beauty and the seeds of
    greatness. But money is something different. We say
    'he was born rich'; but that is precisely what he was
    not. He may have been born into a rich family, of
    rich parents. One is born intelligent or beautiful, but
    not rich. In short, the distribution of money, unlike
    the distribution of intelligence, beauty and the other
    enviable human qualities, is remediable. It is a field
    in which envy can act. The human situation seems to
    the Many outrageous enough without this additional
    unstomachable outrage of vast inequality in the dis-
    tribution of wealth. How dare a millionaire's son be
    the son of a millionaire?

65 The three great historical rejections:
    (a) the rejection of lack of political freedom;
    (b) the rejection of irrational systems of social coste;
    (c) the rejection of gross inequality in wealth.
    The first rejection began with the French Revolution;
    the second is in progress; the third begins.

66 Free enterprise, as we understand it, is to allow a man
    to become as rich as he likes. That is not free enter-
    prise, but free vampirism.

67 The great twentieth-century equation is that I=you.
    And the great twentieth-century envy is that I am less
    than you.

68 Like every other fact, this ubiquitous envy, this desire
    to equalize the wealth of the world, is a utility. Its
    use is obvious: it will force, is already forcing, in the
    form of the Cold War, the richer countries to disgorge
    their wealth, literal and metaphorical.

69 The flaws of a utility are the seeds of its obsoles-
    cence. There are two main flaws in this envy. The
    first is that it is based on the assumption that having
    money and being happy are synonymous. In a capi-
    talist society they very largely are; but this is not in
    the nature of things. It is simply in the nature of a
    capitalist society; and this supposition that wealth is
    the only ticket to happiness, a supposition the capi-
    talist society must encourage if it is to exist, is one
    that will finally enforce profound changes in such
    societies.

70 A capitalist society conditions its members to envy
    and be envied; but this conditioning is a form of
    movement; and the movement will be out of the capi-
    talist society into a better one. I am not saying, as

Marx did, that capitalism contains the seeds of its own destruction; but that it contains the seeds of its own transformation. And that it is high time it started to nurture those seeds.

71 The second flaw in this envy is that it equalizes; and all equalization tends to stagnancy. We must have the equalization, but we do not want the stagnation. This argument from stasis, that inequality is a reservoir of evolutional energy, is one of the most powerful on the side of the advocates of inequality—the rich. Total inequality in wealth, our present condition, is unsatisfactory; and comparative equality of wealth, the situation we are painfully and crotchetily moving into, is full of danger. We need some other eventual situation.*

72 What is this envy, this dreadful groping of the thin fingers of the world's poor for the way of life and the knowledge and the wealth we have over the centuries stored up in the West? It is humanity. Humanity *is* this envy, this desire on the one side to hold, this desire on the other to take. As the mob screams in front of the embassy, as bitter lies foul the wavelength, as the viciously rich grow more selfish and the savagely poor more desperate, as race hates race, as thousands of isolated incidents seem to inflame this last great conflict of man against man, it may seem that this envy is a terrible thing. But I believe, and this is a situation where believing is initially more important than reasoning, that the great sane core of mankind will see this envy for what it really is: a great force to make humanity more human, a situation allowing only one solution—responsibility.

73 What we are before is like a strait, a tricky road, a passage where we need courage and reason. The

courage to go on, not to try to turn back; and the reason to use reason; not fear, not jealousy, not envy, but reason. We must steer by reason, and jettison— because much must go—by reason.

74 Where we are now is where Columbus stood; and looked to sea.

3

THE NEMO

1 I trace all these anxieties back to a supreme source of anguish: that of the nemo.

2 Freud, like arbitrary but convenient Caesar with Gaul, divided the human psyche into three parts, or activities: the *super-ego,* which attempts to control or repress the other two parts; the *ego,* which is the province of conscious desires; and the *id,* which is the obscure chaos of unconscious forces. To Freud the basic energy that both requires the interaction and explains the functions of these three parts of the psyche was the libido, sexual desire, which wells or explodes out of the unconscious, is utilized by the ego and more or less regulated by the super-ego. Most psychologists now recognize that while sexual desire is an important constituent of the raw energy that orientates and fuels our behaviour, it is not the only one. Another very primitive drive is the need for security.

3 But I believe each human psyche has a fourth element, which, using a word indicated by the Freudian terminology, I call the *nemo.* By this I mean not only 'nobody' but also the state of being nobody— 'nobodiness'. In short, just as physicists now postulate an anti-matter, so must we consider the possibility that there exists in the human psyche an anti-ego. This is the nemo.

4 If this concept has not received much attention from

psychologists it may be because it has not, like the other two truly primitive drives of sexual and security (or survival) desire, been with man so long. The desires for sexual satisfaction and security are not even specifically human ones; they are shared by almost all animate matter. But the nemo is a specifically *human* psychic force; a function of civilization, of communication, of the uniquely human ability to compare and hypothesize. Moreover, it is a negative force. We are not, as in the cases of sexual desire and security, attracted towards it; but repelled from it. The superego, ego and id at least seem broadly favourable to the self, and help preserve both individuality and the species. But the nemo is an enemy in the camp.

5 It is not only that we can imagine opposite states, such as the non-existence of the existent thing; we can imagine countless intermediary states. And our nemo gains power over our behaviour to the extent that we believe that were it not for the faults of the human condition, or of society, or of our education, or of our economic position, then we might be what we can imagine. It grows, in short, in strict relation to our sense and knowledge of general and personal inequality.

6 There are basic aspects of the nemo that can never be remedied. I can never be the historical Shakespeare or the historical Cleopatra; I can never be some modern equivalent of them. I can never live for ever . . . and so on. I can imagine myself to be countless things that I shall never be; for I can never be without the physical and psychological defects it is beyond my own, and science's, powers to remedy. Though it is logically nonsensical to call the inevitable a state of inequality, we do in fact think of it so. And this may be termed

the permanent metaphysical sense of the nemo in all of us.

7 The nemo is a man's sense of his own futility and ephemerality; of his relativity, his comparativeness; of his virtual nothingness.

8 All of us are failures; we all die.

9 Nobody wants to be a nobody. All our acts are partly devised to fill or to mask the emptiness we feel at the core.

10 We all like to be loved or hated; it is a sign that we shall be remembered, that we did not 'not exist'. For this reason, many unable to create love have created hate. That too is remembered.

11 The individual thing in front of the whole: my insignificance in face of all that has existed, exists, and will exist. We are almost all dwarfs, and we have the complexes and psychological traits characteristic of dwarfs: feelings of inferiority, with compensatory cunning and malice.

12 We have different ideas of what constitutes a 'somebody'; but there are certain generally accepted specifications. It is necessary to make my name known; I must have power—physical, social, intellectual, artistic, political . . . but power. I must leave monuments, I must be remembered. I must be admired, envied, hated, feared, desired. In short, I must endure, I must extend, and beyond the body and the body's life.

13 Belief in an afterlife is partly an ostrich attempt to cheat the nemo.

14 The new paradise is the entry after death into that
world of the remembered dead where the living continue to wander. One gained access to the old paradise
by good actions and divine grace; but one gains access
to the new paradise simply by actions: actions good
or bad that will be remembered. In the new paradise
the elect are the notorious, the most famous, the
greatest of their kind—whatever that kind was.

15 There are two principal ways to defeat the nemo: I
can conform or I can conflict. If I conform to the
society I live in, I will use the agreed symbols of success, the status symbols, to prove that I am somebody.
Some uniforms prove I am a success; others hide that
I am a failure. One of the attractions of the uniform
is that it puts a man in a situation where part of the
blame for failure can always be put on the group.
A uniform equalizes all who wear it. They all fail
together; if there is success, they all share it.

16 I can counter my nemo by conflicting; by adopting
my own special style of life. I build up an elaborate
unique *persona,* I defy the mass. I am the bohemian,
the dandy, the outsider, the hippy.

17 A great deal of recent art has been conditioned by the
pressures of the nemo. There is the desperate search
for the unique style, and only too often this search
is conducted at the expense of content. Genius will
satisfy both requirements; but many a less gifted contemporary artist has become the victim of his own
'trademark'. This accounts for the enormous proliferation in styles and techniques in our century; and
for that only too characteristic coupling of exoticism
of presentation with banality of theme. Once artists
ran to a centre; now they fly to the circumference.
And the result is our new rococo.

18 One may call this the positive evil effect on art of the
    nemo; but it has also a negative evil one. A jungle of
    pastiche grows round each work or artist that is felt
    to be genuinely 'creative'—that is, nemo-killing.

19 Romantic and post-Romantic art is all pervaded by
    fear of the nemo; by the flight of the individual from
    whatever threatens his individuality. The calm of
    classical statues, classical architecture, classical poetry
    seems noble perhaps, but infinitely remote; and when
    it is without genius, classical art seems to us now
    insipidly bland and monotonously impersonal.

20 At the same time never have so many had such easy
    access to great art. The best is everywhere. The
    smaller we feel, the less able we are to be creative.
    This is why we try to escape through futile new styles,
    futile new fashions, like panic-stricken children in a
    building on fire; throwing ourselves at every exit.

21 We live in an age of short-duration goods. Most of us
    are concerned in the production of such goods. Few
    of us now produce things that will outlast the next
    five years, let alone our lives. We are part of a chain.
    We are nemo-tyrannized.

22 As populations increase, the people that seem to have
    conquered the nemo gain in fascination; and quite
    irrespective of their human worth.

23 Oswald killed President Kennedy in order to kill his
    real enemy: his nemo. He was not a man blind to
    reality, but hypersensitive to it. What drove him to
    kill was the poisonous injustice of both his particular
    society and the whole process. Again and again the
    anarchist assassins of the late nineteenth century
    asserted this: they did what they did to make them-

selves equal with the assassinated. One said: 'Now I shall be remembered as long as he is.'*

24 The German people allowed Hitler to dominate their lives for the same reason. Like individuals, races and countries can lose their sense of importance, of meaningfulness. A great dictator is like a uniform; he gives the illusion to all below him that the nemo is defeated.

25 On a less harmful level we see it in the mass admiration of the famous and the successful; of the film star, the 'personality', the 'celebrity'; in the popularity of the gossip magazine, the pin-up cult, the cheap biography, in the imitative mannerisms and living-styles disseminated by women's magazines. We see it in the attention lavished on every flashy mediocrity, every mayfly success. It is not only Hollywood that treats everything it produces as 'great': the public wants this spurious greatness.

26 The nemo is strongest in the most evolved and best educated, weakest in the most primitive and ignorant. So it is clear that its power can only increase, not only as higher general standards of education are achieved, but also as the populations of the world grow. To the extent that there is more opportunity for leisure and more information available, boredom and envy will also increase. Terrible chain-reactions come into play: the more individuals the less individual they each feel; the more clearly they see injustice and inequality the more helpless they seem to become; the more they know the more they want to be known; and the more they want to be known the less likely it becomes that they will be.

27 As it becomes increasingly difficult to defeat the nemo by attracting attention in the outside world, we turn

increasingly to the small personal world in which we live: to friends, relations, neighbours, colleagues. If we can defeat the nemo there, then that at least is something; and so arises the current obsession with conspicuous consumption, with keeping up with the Joneses, with proving our superiority on however absurd and humble a level—in our skill with a golf-club, with Italian cooking, with growing roses. So arises our mania for gambling in all its forms; and even our pre-occupation with things excellent in themselves, like higher wages and healthier and better-educated children.

28 But the most common refuge against the nemo is the marriage, the family, the home. Children, the long-walk of the blood, are the real life-insurance. Yet the nemo may cause abuse in this situation. It may force the individual to act the part at home that he or she cannot act in public and can act only otherwise in the world of dreams. The would-be dictator becomes the domestic dictator; the remembered in this room. It may force parents to be tyrants; the husband or wife into infidelity. There is no commoner flight from the nemo than into a forbidden bed.

29 The ordinary man and woman live in an asphyxiating smog of opinions foisted on them by society. They lose all independence of judgement and all freedom of action. They see themselves increasingly as limited special functions, as parts of a machine, with neither need nor right to perform any other than their role in the economic structure of society. The civic sense becomes atrophied. It is the job of the police to prevent crimes, not yours or mine; it is the job of the town councillor to run the town, not yours or mine; it is the job of the underprivileged to fight for their rights, not yours or mine. Thus more and more live in

cities, and yet more and more become decitizenized.
What began in the suburbs reaches right to the city's
heart.

THE POLITICAL NEMO

30   The atrophy of the civic sense is one of the most
striking social phenomena of our age. Man is a political being; and this atrophy is caused by the fact that
however successful we may be in other fields in dealing with the nemo, we are all almost no more than
helpless cogs in the political machine.

31   We have no political power at all. This is not a new
state of affairs, but there is a new quasi-existentialist
awareness that the state exists.

32   In the world as it is, democracy, the right of any sane
adult to vote freely for the freely-elected candidate of
a freely-constituted party with a freely-evolved policy,
is the best system. It is the best system not because it
will necessarily produce the best régime, but because
it gives most freedom of choice to beings whose most
urgent need is freedom of choice. No electorate, if
allowed to choose, will choose the same general policy
unanimously. This key political reality, based on the
fact that there is no economic equality anywhere in
the world, means that any régime maintaining that the
right choice of general policy is so obvious that the
electorate need not and should not be given the opportunity to vote for any other policy is a danger nation-
ally and internationally; and this is so even when the
régime is demonstrably right in its choice of policy.
It is a national danger mainly because it is also an
international one.

33   The Platonic republic could impose humanity and

nobility on its citizens, but this very imposition of what might have been freely expressed on what might have freely expressed it immediately sets up a tension that vitiates the theoretical goodness of the measures imposed. I can stick artificial flowers on this tree that will not flower; or I can create the conditions in which the tree is likely to flower naturally. I may have to wait longer for my real flowers, but they are the only true ones.

34 Democracy tries to give choice to as many as possible, and this is its saving virtue; but the wider the franchise and the larger the population grows, the sharper becomes the irony.

35 A few dozen act while millions stand impotent.

36 That everyone has the vote is a general guarantee of some sort of freedom; but it means nothing in itself. My vote influences nothing, decides nothing. Whether I vote or not is immaterial.

37 I vote because not to vote represents a denial of the principle of right of franchise; but not because voting in any way relieves my sense that I am a pawn, and a smaller and smaller pawn, as the electorate grows.

38 An informed man of fifty is the equal at the polling booth of a shopgirl who left school when she was fifteen and knows no more of the real issues on which she is voting than a parrot. They must, to satisfy democracy, be equal at the polling booth; the informed man of fifty would probably be the first to say so. Yet there is a cruelty in this situation, an irony, and an absurdity. An intelligent man is not the same as an ignoramus; yet this is what the polling booth says.

39 A common result of this necessary yet merciless
    equality; I have no real say in the way the society and
    country I live in are run; I will do for them what they
    force me by law to do; but all the rest of my energy
    and resources will be for my private ends. This sense
    of total non-participation, of being a pawn in the
    hands of the chess players, the governors and minis-
    ters, is seemingly paralleled in the cosmic situation;
    and our view of that situation is coloured, darkly,
    by our view of our virtually non-existent part in the
    government of our own country.

40 My vote is a futile scrap of paper tossed in a great
    river; and my life seems a futile atom lost in the end-
    less flux. Resentment becomes pragmatic; egocentric-
    ity, logical; and the expression of political feeling by
    illegal and dangerous means—anarchy, rioting, sub-
    version—inevitable.

41 There is only one practical way of lessening this
    pawn complex and that is by adding to the usual
    definition of democracy (the right of all adults to vote
    freely) the rider 'and as frequently as is conveniently
    possible'. We can now certainly cope with the tech-
    nological and social problems of a more frequent
    general vote on great national issues; and in most
    Western countries we can, or could, provide the
    indispensable safeguards of a free press and an un-
    biassed service of information together with a suffi-
    ciently high general standard of education to com-
    prehend and assess it.

42 The one group of people who would certainly reject
    this idea are the politicians themselves, although they
    increasingly pay attention to what is a form of un-
    official (and dangerously manipulatable) plebiscite:
    the opinion poll. Their arguments are familiar—the

fickleness and emotional nature of public opinion, the impossibility of governing without continuity of policy, the need to keep secret certain factors in decision-making, and so on. These arguments are not without reason. But men in power are never wholly disinterested in retaining power. However much they may disagree with their opponents over policy, they will agree on the rules of the power game; who gets control may fight tooth and nail to keep it.

43 The public is woman before emancipation. If she was fickle and emotional in her decisions it was because she had never been allowed or expected or conditioned to be anything else; and just as this was a dangerous situation for society, so is the present total non-participation in government by the vast majority of adults.

44 A more frequent vote system would not greatly alleviate the individual predicament, which is strictly a numerical one. The single vote must always count for nothing. But it is the first step towards a less isolating situation. Meanwhile, we shall remain the impotent millions.

THE NECESSITY OF THE NEMO

45 And yet the nemo, like hazard, like the indifference of the process to the individual, is essential to man. It is the effect in him of knowing that human existence is unequal. It is both the passive horror of this condition and the active source of the energy needed to remedy it.

46 The nemo is an evolutionary force, as necessary as the ego. The ego is certainty, what I am; the nemo is

potentiality, what I am not. But instead of utilizing the nemo as we would utilize any other force, we allow ourselves to be terrified by it, as primitive man was terrified by lightning. We run screaming from this mysterious shape in the middle of our town, even though the real terror is not in itself, but in our terror at it.

4

RELATIVITY OF RECOMPENSE

1 If we allow ourselves to be trapped between the jaws of our imagination and our reality—between that better world we dream of and the worse one we inhabit—we may find our condition a very unsatisfactory one; and one of our traditional compensations is to look down at all those 'lower' forms of life to which we suppose ourselves superior in happiness. Our human world may seem cruel and brief; but in the rest of nature at least it is worse. This consolation does not bear close scrutiny, for what is revealed then is not a universe of hazard-bestowed privilege, one in which man stands highest on the ladder of luck, but one in which—with a single exception—there reigns a mysterious balance and *equality* among all the forms of animate matter. I call this equality in existing *relativity of recompense.*

2 It can be defined thus: *Relativity of recompense is that which allows, at any stage of evolution, any sentient creature to find under normal conditions the same comparative pleasure in existing as all other sentient creatures of its own or any other age.* Two factors establish this equality among all sentient forms of life, whether they be past or present, simple or complex, with a life-span of an hour or one of decades. The first is that they are all able to feel pleasure and pain; the second is that not one of them is able to compare its own experience of pleasure and pain with any other creature's. The single exception to this happy oblivion is man.

59

3   But if man is an exception it is in relation to his own age, not to past or future ages. That there are 'perfect' and 'imperfect' stages of evolution is, from the point of view of the pleasure to be derived from being, a mirage. There is no justification for saying that in general the humanity of our own age is happier or less happy than the humanity of any or some other age, past or future. We have no means of assessing the intensity of the pleasure other ages found or will find in existing; and it is certain that whole sources of pleasure and modes of feeling, like whole species, can fall extinct. This vitiates any calculation of special absolute recompense.

4   Our world may seem more secure, another may have seemed more adventurous. Our world may seem more knowledgeable; another, more full of mystery. There is no apparent special advantage of our age that cannot be balanced by some special advantage in every other.

5   All life lies parallel in each moment of time. In the scale of happiness evolution is horizontal, not vertical.

6   All dogs, past, present and future, are equally happy. It is clear to us humans that they are not; but no dog knows this. Man then has been exiled from contemporary relativity of recompense by consciousness. The enormous price of knowledge is the power to imagine and the consequent power to compare. The 'golden' age was the age before comparison; and if there had been a Garden of Eden and a Fall, they would have been when man could not compare and when he could: between *Genesis 3:6* and *Genesis 3:7*.

7   Every human object of envy raises two doubts. Is he as happy in his circumstances as I imagine him to be? Would I be as happy in his circumstances as I imagine I would? These doubts should lessen the effects of inequality. But the capitalist notion that the conditions of happiness are the same for all tends to make us answer each doubt in the affirmative.

8   The millionaire buying a luxury yacht; the commuter buying a new car; the workman buying a new fishing rod; the hobo getting a sound pair of shoes. It is axiomatic in a capitalist society that hobo envies workman envies commuter envies millionaire. It is lucky for those who believe in such societies that we know neither the degrees of pleasure nor where we each stand against them. But man still gropes after that remote memory of the animal relativity of recompense. Although we may not, in terms of individual pleasure felt, be quite so far from it as we are led to imagine in a money-worshipping society, we are far enough.

9   Humanity, though exiled from relativity of recompense by the development of consciousness and imagination, has, by this very development, the power to institute a conscious and rational contemporary relativity of the same kind. For us the lack of relativity of recompense, the inequality we know, is the prime reason for progress. We are allowed to see that we are not equally recompensed; and far from it. *But we are the only organism that can know, tolerate the knowledge, and find the remedy.*

10 Animals lack what we have gained, but we have lost what they still have. We should love them not for their human attributes, but for their innocence. With

them we are still in the Garden of Eden; and with ourselves the Fall is every day.

11 The forms of non-human animate life are like a gang of builders in absolute darkness, unable to see either their own or their fellows' work. But we were given light to see by; and at once we saw that some had easier and pleasanter work than others, and there began the long age of envy. But now slowly we realize, we must realize, that we all deserve access to, even if we do not get, equal happiness. The message of our situation is clear: we must create the same equality in the new light as we were given in the old darkness.

12 We have no guarantee that humanity is not an aberration of evolution, a doomed sideline. At most we can be only an experiment, a possibility in the process. Consciousness has given us the power to destroy ourselves as well as the power to preserve ourselves. Nothing shows more clearly that to be human is not a privilege, but an irrelevance to all except humanity.

HAPPINESS AND ENVY

13 We measure the amount of inequality in our personal and social lives by the concepts of happiness and envy. These two conditions dominate our behaviour, and we can trace their origins back to the most primitive forms of life. Happiness is to possess the means of survival—'territory', 'cover', a mate, food, effective means of defence against predators and parasites, and so on; envy is to lack these things. Happiness, in short, is security, but a security defined by the experience of insecurity, which is the passive aspect of envy.

14 Happiness is essentially the desire to prolong life just
as it is; envy, to change it. In terms of evolution happiness is thus a chief obstacle to progress; and envy, a
chief source of it. Yet happiness is a kind of proof
that it was worth surviving *until* now, just as envy
is a kind of intention to survive *from now on.*
Both states are necessary for evolution. One is the
propaganda department publicizing past and present
achievements of the government, and the other is a
permanent committee of criticism.

15 Plato's definition of the just society was one in which
each is happy to be what he or she is; that is, a society
without envy. In our unjust ones, all our political and
social confrontations are between the party of happiness and the party of envy; and all our present
troubles stem from our inability to think of these two
parties except as mutually destructive opposites whose
only postures can be those of aggression.

16 Happiness is essentially anti-social. It always implies
a comparison, a knowing that others could be, but
are not, enjoying the particular happiness that we
enjoy. This is true of private happiness and public
happiness. The theatre audience, the stadium of spectators, even a whole nation are happy because there
are others not present and not happy in this way.

17 Happiness is that it happens to me, and the happiness
of even the poorest man is unique; he can only be
envied it. It is and can be only his. We are all
Crusoes; no one knows our happiness, and unhappiness, like ourselves.

18 It is therefore in the nature of happiness to create an
unequal world. A source of happiness available to all
becomes like a woman available to all; possession be-

25 Our problem is to reconstruct the relativity of recompense of our pre-conscious past; to isolate the virtues of both envy and happiness, to take the destructive aggression from the one and the destructive selfishness from the other, and to get them to interact. Above all, it is to establish this by science and reason and charity, and not by emotion, blood and blackmail.

5

DOING THE GOOD

1 There remains one other, and very vital, problem that breeds dissatisfaction with the human condition. It is freedom of will.

2 We are here in another Bet Situation; that is, we are faced with a problem that we cannot and never shall solve, but about which we ought to come to some conclusion. I must bet either that I have no freedom of will and my actions are never my own, however free and willed they appear to be, or I must bet that I have, or can achieve, some sort of freedom. I can, thirdly, make no bet and remain agnostic.

3 This is in many ways an easier race to bet on than those that oppose an intervening and a non-intervening god, or an afterlife and a total extinction. Most religions and codes of justice have supposed complete freedom of will in order to make their ethical and punitive systems effective; and this is more forgiveable, if no less undemonstrable than the determinist reduction of all human behaviour to mechanics. 'A mailman was drowned in the floods' and 'A mailman was murdered by a gunman' may belong to the same category of events in evolution; but not in their significance to human society. We may say that this particular murderer had no freedom of choice when he pressed the trigger; but not that all men would have had no choice in a similar situation. We may argue about the degree of free will possessed by this or that individual; but to deny it to all mankind is to beg the

great question of why we are not all gunmen—and why we are capable of disinterested choices.

4 It may turn out finally that indeed we do not, in some evolutionary or biological sense, possess any free will. All our 'free' choices may be finally attributable to some conditioning over which we have no control. Even if we could establish the contrary—total free will—we are still limited, since to be completely free we should need an absolutely free field of choice as well as the freedom to choose in it. We are in fact confined to the courses of action available, perceivable and feasible to us. I cannot choose whether to be a woman or not because I was born male; and so on. Yet there remains the fact that we all have experience of situations when we *feel* (and more importantly, an outside observer can feel) we choose freely. We are perhaps, are almost certainly, machines; but we are machines so complex that they have developed a relative freedom to choose. We are in a prison cell, but it is, or can be made to become, a comparatively spacious one; and inside it we can become relatively free.

5 There may be situations and senses in which Euclidean geometry is not true; but it is enough for ordinary purposes that it seems true, and 'works', in ordinary situations.

6 Chess permits freedom of permutations within a framework of set rules and prescribed movements. Because a chess player cannot move *absolutely* as he likes, either in terms of the rules or in terms of the exigencies of the particular game, has he no freedom of move? The separate game of chess I play with existence has different rules from your and every other game; the only similarity is that each of our separate

games always has rules. The gifts, inherited and acquired, that are special to me are the rules of the game; and the situation I am in at any given moment is the situation of the game. My freedom is the choice of action and the power of enactment I have within the rules and situation of the game.

7 There is finally a paradoxical sense in which we gain free will by living in society. At the most obvious level, the final decision of a committee, though it may not be the decision that some individual members would have arrived at 'of their own free will', does represent a freedom of general human will in the face of an apparently determining biological system. This is perhaps the deepest psychological attraction society holds for the individual; though the more easily comprehensible individual in each of us tends to think of other people's opinions and beliefs as in some way hostile and confining, a deeper intelligence in each is aware that what springs out of this conflict is a greater general freedom—and one in which each eventually shares.

'GRATUITOUS ACTS'

8 A famous category of actions—'gratuitous acts' or sudden decisions without rational motivation—are supposed to prove absolute freedom of will. But all they prove is contempt for convention. They spring from the heresy that all restriction is analogous to imprisonment; as if everything we know, from the observable cosmos to the meson, is not restricted.

9 If I were to throw a rotten egg at the Archbishop of Canterbury I might prove that I have no respect for convention; but I prove nothing about freedom of

will. A world of irrational actions would not constitute an absolutely free world because for human beings anarchy is only freedom when everyone wants anarchy.

10 In a world where the individual is, or feels that he is, being stamped out of existence it is only natural that the gratuitous act should gain a certain glamour. But this is an indictment of the world as it is, not a justification of the gratuitous act, or a proof of free will.

THE PURPOSE OF RELATIVE FREEDOM

11 If we are only relatively free, then it must be so that we shall evolve a greater relative freedom. This freedom is something that has to be gained: both by the individual in his own lifetime, and by the species during its long history.

12 It is obvious what it is gained by: greater intelligence and greater knowledge, both of self and of life. In practical social terms it requires a higher general standard of education and a different kind of education. Above all it requires social equality. Freedom of will is strictly related to freedom of living condition.

INABILITY TO ENACT GOOD

13 Since it is essential that we should fail to do evil, it is necessary that we should sometimes fail to do good. Will is an amoral force, like electricity: it can kill or it can serve. Failure to enact represents an indispensable safety system, like the fuses in an electrical system.

14 Even if we could enact more of what we willed, the world would be no better since the increased power to will and enact would apply to both good and evil actions. Therefore, to say that we wish we could enact what we will is to say that we need more training in determining what is good and what is evil; not in willing and enacting.

15 Animals have strong wills; they try to enact whatever they will. They are incapable of not acting as they will. That is how we trap them. Weak-willedness both oils and safeguards the machine of human society.

16 But our dissatisfaction is that we are unable to enact the good we freely will. I have a shilling in my pocket for this charity box; yet I pass it by. There are six principle causes of such failure.

17 The *first* stems from the fatalist belief that we have no freedom of choice in willing an action; and therefore we enact, if we enact, what is chosen for us. Our choosing is an illusion; our action, a waste of energy. To do or not to do . . . who cares?

18 The *second* cause of failure to enact good stems from conflict of intention. High intelligence leads to multiplicity of interest and a sharpened capacity to foresee the consequences of any action. Will is lost in a labyrinth of hypothesis.

19 All forks dream of crossroads; in atoms as in men, complexification causes loss of energy. Throughout history the intelligentsia have been despised for their weakness as enactors. But it would be only in a world where high intelligence were synonymous with high morality that one could wish the most intelligent to have the most power.

20   The *third* cause of failure to enact good stems from our ability to imagine fulfilment. We know from experience that things rarely turn out as pleasantly as we imagined they might have done; and an imagined ideal consequence may take such a hold on our minds that it becomes impossible to risk the disappointments of reality.

21   Before I act it is as if I had acted before. To *say* you believe in doing something may be, except in front of witnesses likely to hold you to your word, merely to give yourself an excuse not to do it. For *goodness is action; not intention to act.*

22   Before it is performed every action requiring a conscious effort of will (that is, which is not obligatory or instinctive) is to the imagination like a sleeping princess. It lies at the heart of an enchanted forest of potentialities. The actual performance then threatens to destroy all that might have been created by other actions; and there is a close parallel with the sexual situation. It is more pleasurable to prolong the time before ejaculation. It is nice to be mean today because I shall be generous tomorrow.

23   The *fourth* cause of failure to enact good stems from the desire to prove to ourselves by not acting that we can choose to act. Not to act is to act. I am what I do not do, as well as what I do. The refusal to act is often equivalent to the gratuitous act. Its fundamental motive is to prove I am free.

24   The *fifth* cause of failure to enact is that the action contemplated is so small in relation to the final intention that it seems pointless. It is between these tiny stools—moving the Sahara grain by grain, spooning

out the Atlantic—that so many good causes vanish into thin air.

25 The *sixth* cause of failure to enact applies to those actions that are against something. Here the mechanism of countersupporting may prevent action.

COUNTERSUPPORTING

26 If I am attracted strongly towards a moral or aesthetic or politico-social pole, I shall hate and may wish to suppress its counterpole. But I shall also know that the pole under whose positive influence I live is dependent for much of its energy on that counterpole; furthermore, I derive pleasure from being attracted. My opposition to the counterpole will in this case frequently be of a peculiar kind. I call this kind of opposition *countersupporting.*

27 I may offer violent physical opposition to some idea or social tendency. But violence breeds violence; strength breeds strength; resource breeds resource. Violent persecution often conceals a desire that enough of the persecuted shall survive for the exercise of more violence. Fox hunters preserve foxes. The keenest shots preserve game most keenly.

28 Violence strengthens the opposed; passion tempers it. To argue passionately against something is to give it passion.

29 Games were invented as a kind of *perpetuum mobile,* an eternal receptacle for human energy. All the great games: animal baiting, hunting, fishing, ball games, chess, cards, dice, all admit of endless permutations.

A great game is an unfailing well; and it is precisely
this inexhaustibility that the countersupporter seeks
in the enemy. The Anglo-Saxon ethic of sportsman-
ship and fair play, which developed out of *amour
courtois* notions of chivalry, enshrines very clearly
the principle of countersupporting.*

30   *Purely* emotive opposition is a boomerang—it will
always return home, and not simply to roost. Any
opposition that can be picked up and used by the
enemy in return is not opposition, but countersupport.

31   The most current way of countersupporting is by
masked toleration. It is a general innate weakness of
high intelligence. I show actionless hostility towards a
counterpole; it is generally one of so vast and general
a nature that it seems that however active I might be
I could have no effect on the situation as a whole.

32   The masked tolerator knows that the thing he opposes is essential to his well-being. He may, indeed
usually does, enjoy expressing his opposition verbally,
but he rarely makes any constructive opposing *action*.
Very often he will despise the active workers of the
cause that publicly fight what he opposes. He will say
that such people are pursuing private ends—they like
the excitement of action, they are born extroverts—
and that he himself sees too deep, too far. He knows
the vanity, or futility, or illusoriness, of active opposition. This is the most felt, most shared, most enjoyed
despair of our age.

33   The artistic figures considered most significant in and
of our century are those that best express this conscious sense of fact of intellectual will-lessness and
inadequacy—the fallen saint, the weak man; and

those that express the potent contrary—the men of action, the doers. Think of the Wild Western hero; the characters in Beckett and Greene, Hemingway and Malraux.

34   The Don Quixotes of our modern La Mancha are those duped by the myth that to oppose must mean to wish to destroy; and that to be unable to destroy is a tragic situation.

35   There are two motives in all opposition; and the two motives are antipathetic. One is rightly or wrongly the will to suppress all opposition, the other is rightly or wrongly the will to prolong it. It is necessary to determine before opposing what part these two wills play.

36   There are more kinds of hypocrisy than the conscious ones. All opposition points to the opposed. Look how attractive Christianity has made sin. The best opposition is always scientific, logical, rational. The more unanswerable in reason it is, the better it is.

37   The psychiatric patient is not cured, but made less abnormal, by understanding the contradictions of his own nature. Dimly he begins to see how the forces that use him can be used. To understand is not only to forgive; it is to control.

38   Before opposing, ask these questions:
     To what extent do I enjoy opposing?
     If I could annihilate in one blow all that I oppose, would I make that blow?
     Will my opposition weaken or strengthen the thing opposed?
     How effective is my proposed form of opposition likely to be?
     Is it a pose or a reality?

To what extent is it caused purely by a desire to be admired, or not despised, by those I admire?

Is there anything else I could oppose more usefully?

39   My opposition is 'my duty'; if I once admitted that my opposition was really my pleasure . . .

40   Tears wept on enemy graves are often peculiarly sincere; we weep our own now homeless energy.

41   So many movements of opposition are Charges of the Light Brigade. And, symptomatically, we admire their failure more than we hate their waste and futility.

GOOD EQUALS EVIL

42   There is one last desperate argument sometimes advanced against doing good actions. It is this: all actions, whether intended to be good or bad, interweave so extensively as time passes that finally their relative goodness or badness completely disappears. Both evil and good die; or are metamorphosed.

43   We all know evils to some can cause good to others; but to leap from what may be true of the whole, or true of any given action viewed historically, to the theory that the individual can be excused any moral concern about his actions is to fall into the fallacy that what is true of an action must be true of the enactor. A man must finally do good for his own and his society's health; not for good's sake or the action's sake.

44   If good finally becomes lost in evil, and evil in good, then it is to ensure the survival of matter; not of humanity.

45 All our judgements of right and wrong are absolutely
and evolutionally meaningless. But we are like a judge
who is compelled to judge. Our function is to judge,
to choose between good and evil. If we refuse to do
so, we cease to be human beings and revert to our
basic state, of being matter; and even at his very
worst the very worst among us is still something more
than a few score kilograms of complaisant molecules.

WIIY SO LITTLE GOOD?

46 Yet even given these reasons, given that failure to
enact good must often arise from the difficulty of
knowing which of several possible courses *is* the best
or from a genuine inability to see any necessity for
action (the ancient heresy of quietism), we are all
aware that we do not do all the good we could. However stupid we are, there are simple situations in
which we can see a clearly good course of action,
and yet shirk it; however selfish we are, there are
good courses that involve no self-sacrifice, and yet we
shirk them.

47 For the last two and a half millennia almost every
great thinker, every great saint, every great artist has
advocated, personified and celebrated— or at least implied—the nobility and excellence of the good act as
the basis of the just society. On their evidence its
social and biological value cannot be in doubt. So it
almost seems as if the great humans are wrong, as if
in the commoner bulk of mankind there was some
apprehension of a perverse but deeper truth: it is
better generally to do nothing than generally to do
good.

48 I believe this strange and irrational apathy is largely

due to the religion-engendered myths that doing good will bring us pleasure—if there is an after-life, eternal pleasure—and that thus the good man is *happier* than the bad. The world around us is full of evidence that these are indeed myths: good men are very often far less happy than bad ones, and good actions very often bring nothing but pain. Just as he is an eternal seeker of the agent, man is an eternal seeker of the reward. He feels there ought to be some further recompense —something more than a clear conscience and a feeling of self-righteousness—for doing good. The conclusion is irresistible: doing good must bring (and therefore before the doing, promise) pleasure. If it does not, then it is a bad bargain.

49 There are two obvious 'modes' of pleasure. One we may call *intended* in that the event which brings pleasure, the meeting with a lover, the visit to a concert, is planned and intended. The second and much more important kind is *fortuitous,* in that it comes unexpectedly—not only the surprise meeting with an old friend, the sudden beauty of some usually banal landscape, but all those elements in the active intention to have pleasure that were not clearly foreseen. In fact, when we plan an intended pleasure we always unconsciously assume that there will be a free bonus of the fortuitous kind. Our approach is that of the traveller: to the extent that his journey is planned and has definite aims he will get the pleasure intended, but he will also expect a very large content of the fortuitous kind, both in what he intended to happen to him and in what will happen to him by chance. In this way we hedge our bets—if the planned pleasures disappoint, there are the unexpected ones, and vice versa.

50 What is immediately striking about both these modes of pleasure is that they depend very largely on hazard.

A girl may have long planned to marry. But when the wedding is finally present, is taking place, there is a sense of good luck. Nothing has happened, although many things could have happened, to prevent it. Perhaps she may look back then to the chance first encounter with the man who is now her husband; and the basic element of hazard there is overwhelming. In short, we are conditioned to see pleasure of both kinds as very largely a result of hazard. *We do not arrive at it so much as it arrives at us.*

51 But as soon as we treat pleasure as a kind of successful bet, and then expect this sort of pleasure from moral choices and actions, we are in trouble. The atmosphere of chance that pervades the one world will contaminate the other. Hazard rules the laws of pleasure—so let it, we say, rule the laws of doing good. Worse than that we shall come to the obvious conclusion that only good actions that promise pleasure are worth our doing. The pleasure may come from community esteem, from personal gratitude, from self-interest (the hope of good in return); from hopes of a pleasant afterlife; from being freed of the sense of guilt, if such a sense has been 'built in' by the cultural environment. But in each case the incentive, however necessary historically or justifiable on pragmatic grounds, creates a totally wrong climate around our intention to act well.

52 *Doing good for some public reward is not doing good: it is doing something for public reward.* That it also does good may seem to be its justification; but it is a dangerous justification, as I shall show.

53 There is a third less obvious 'mode' of pleasure to which we do not usually attach the idea, though we have the sensation, of pleasure. We may call it *func-*

tional, and it is the pleasure we get from all those activities essential to our being—eating, excreting, breathing, and ultimately, existing. In a sense these are the only pleasures we cannot deny having. If we do not distinguish them very clearly it is because they are overlaid by the other two much more conscious and complex modes. If I choose what I eat, I experience the intended pleasure; if I enjoy what I eat more than I expected, I experience the fortuitous; but buried beneath is the functional pleasure of eating because to eat is to continue to exist. To use Jungian terminology, this third mode is archetypal, and I believe that from it we ought to derive our motive for doing good. In terms of bodily functions, we should *evacuate* good—not *ejaculate* it.

54 We never have a surfeit of natural bodily functions. We expect no extrinsic reward for carrying them out, since we know that the reward lies in the performance. Non-performance means illness or death, just as the non-performance of good actions finally means the death of society. Charity, kindness to others, actions against injustice and inequality should be *acts of hygiene, not of pleasure.*

55 What then does the functional 'health' thus brought about consist of? Its most important element is this: that the good action (and from 'good action' I am here excluding all those actions whose real motive is public esteem) is the most convincing proof we shall ever have that we do possess a relative freedom of will. Even when it does not involve acting against our self-interest, the good action requires a lack of self-interest, or conversely, an output of unnecessary (in terms of our biological needs) energy. It is an act against inertia, against what would have been otherwise determined by inertia and natural process. In a

sense it is a divine act, in the old sense of divine: that is, the intervention of a free will upon matter imprisoned in its mere matterness.

56 *All our concepts of God are concepts of our own potentialities.* The charity and compassion that have been universally attributed to the finest—under their different outward masks—of such God-concepts are the qualities we are striving to establish in ourselves. They have nothing to do with any external 'absolute' reality; they are reflections of our hopes.

57 We cannot in ordinary life easily separate self-interested motives from the 'hygienic' one I propose. But the hygienic motive can always be used to assess the others. It constitutes a check upon them, and especially in that sadly wide category where the action seems good in the enactor's mind but is clearly evil in its effects. There were certainly members of the Inquisition, there were Protestant witch-burners, there were perhaps even Nazi race-exterminators who genuinely and disinterestedly believed in the goodness of what they were doing. But even if one gives them every benefit of every doubt, they were all impelled by spurious rewards for their 'good' actions. They hoped for a better world to come *for themselves* and their co-believers, not for the heretics, witches and Jews they destroyed. *They acted not for greater freedom, but for greater pleasure.*

58 Freedom of will in a world without freedom is like a fish in a world without water. It cannot exist because it cannot use itself. The greatest fallacy of political tyranny has always been that the tyrant is free while his subjects are enslaved; but he is enslaved by his own enslaving, tyrannized by his own tyranny. He is not free to act as he wishes because what he wishes

is determined, and generally very narrowly, by the demands of maintaining tyranny. And this political truth is true on a personal level. If the intention of a good action is not finally to institute more freedom (therefore, more justice and equality) for all, it will be partly evil not only to the object of the action but to the enactor, since its evil aspects will limit his own freedom. In terms of functional pleasure, it will be similar to unexcreted food, whose nutritional goodness is progressively counteracted by the damage it will do if its harmful elements are not passed out of the organism.

59 Over the last two hundred years there has been a great improvement in personal and public hygiene and cleanliness; and this was largely brought about by persuading people that the results of being dirty and apathetic in the face of disease were not acts of God, but preventable acts of nature; not the sheer misery in things, but the controllable mechanisms of life.

60 We have had the first, the physical, phase of the hygienic revolution; it is time we went to the barricades for the second, the mental. Not doing good when you usefully could is not immoral; it is going about with excrement on the hands.

6

THE TENSIONAL NATURE OF

HUMAN REALITY

1 Because of our powers of reasoning, imagining and
   supposing, we exist mentally in a world of opposites,
   converses, negatives. There may be some kind of absolute reality that is not like this. There may be other
   relative realities. But this tensional, or polar, reality is
   the one we humans inhabit.

2 Anything that exists or can be imagined to exist is a
   pole. All feelings, ideas, thoughts, are poles; and each
   pole has counterpoles.

3 There are two categories of counterpole. One is nothingness, the non-existence of the pole. The other is
   whatever denies, attacks, diminishes, stands contrary
   to or diverts from the pole.

4 The obvious counterpole of an idea is the contrary
   idea. *The world is round; the world is not round.* But
   whatever else stands between my mind and its con-
   tinuous concentration on the idea (*The world is
   round*) is also a counterpole. Now the contrary idea
   (*The world is not round*) is at first sight the most
   dangerous enemy of the pole idea; but all those subsidiary counterpoles (other concerns, other events,
   other exigencies, other ideas) that distract the mind
   from the pole idea endanger it far more; in fact, to
   the extent that they do not signal it, but submerge it,
   they reduce it to nothingness. There is thus a para-

doxical sense in which the contrary idea signals and supports the idea to which it is superficially most opposed.

5 Even when contrary propositions are meaningless or demonstrably false they contribute life and meaning to the propositions they oppose; just as the non-existence, in human terms of existing, of 'God' gives life and meaning to all that exists.

6 Our first and most direct apprehension of this polarity is got from our experience of our own self—our body and then our mind.

THE COUNTERPOLES OF THE 'I'

7 I am made constantly aware of the otherness of things. They are all in some sense my counterpoles. A Sartrean existentialist would say that they hedge me in, they tyrannize me, they encroach on my selfhood. But they define me, they tell me what I am, and if I am not told what I am, I do not know what I am. I am aware too that all other objects are in exactly the same situation as myself: minute pole in a vast ocean of counterpoles, I am infinitely isolated, but my situation is infinitely repeated.

8 All parts of my body are objects external to me: my hands, my tongue, my digestive mechanism. The words I speak are counterpoles. There is no mental activity I cannot stand back from and be towards as to a counterpole. So I am a tissue of counterpoles. My body and my thoughts and my words are like the garden and the rooms and the furniture of my house. Certainly they seem to me more mine than your gar-

den or the room you read in at this moment; but a moment's analysis tells me that they are not mine in any total or scientific sense. They are mine in the artificiality of the law, and in the illogicality (or bio-logicality) of emotion. My garden is this collection of grass, earth, plants, trees that I possess in law and can enjoy while I live; it is not mine. Nothing, not even what I call my self, is mine; individuality and coun-ter-polarity separate me from all.

9   I see these strange tools, my hands, at the end of my arms; I see these strange tools, my arms, that hang from my shoulders; I see these strange tools, my shoulders, that curve from my neck; I see this strange tool, my neck, that carries my head; I see this strange tool, my head, that holds my brain; I see this strange tool, my brain, that sees itself and calls itself a tool and tries to find in itself a thing not a tool that it is a tool for.

10 Where then is the ultimate pole? Where is the 'I' that permits me to make these descriptions? Which claims that everything, both in and outside me, is other? Plainly, it is no more than a recording of phenomena; a colourless mechanism distinguished from other such mechanisms only by its position in space and time. Ultimately 'I' is simply the common condition of all human mentality.

11 The description we habitually make is this: 'I am aware of this disturbance that has happened in my brain.' But it is more accurate to say: 'This disturb-ance disturbed and the disturbing took place in the particular field of experience that the reflector of the disturbance, the stater of this statement, exists in.' 'I' is thus a convenient geographical description, not an absolute entity.

12 If the 'I' pole is anything it is the sum of reflected (and recollected) disturbances in this field. If there had been no disturbances there would be no 'mirror'; no 'I'. In short, 'I' is constituted by its counterpoles; without them it is nothing.

13 There is however a sense in which each counterpole must seem hostile to the 'ghost' called 'I' that has been constituted by all other counterpoles. The directly contrary counterpole to *I am* is *I am not*. That is paradoxically not the most hostile since my death (as tombstones remind us) at least signals my existence. The way in which we ordinarily think of our own death is not morbid; on the contrary, one of the simplest ways of assuring ourselves that we live. But the counterpoles that are external to my body and my immediate surroundings and possessions are all in effect submergers of me. They distract my (and other people's) concentration from myself. They diminish me. And thus they give rise to my personal sense of nemo.

14 What we consciously or subconsciously require of a counterpole is that it in some way signals and confirms our existence; because we own it in law, because it loves us or hates us or needs us or acknowledges us; because we can identify ourselves either with it or, by the process of countersupporting, *against* it. The more we are aware of the nothingness at the still centre of our being—that nothingness we mask by talking of 'I'—the more we look for these ego-reflective (or nemo-destructive) qualities in the counterpoles with which we can choose to furnish our lives.

15 Between all these counterpoles, both choosable and inevitable, and the 'I' pole there exists a relationship;

but since the counterpoles are in themselves poles and have their own counterpoles (one of which is constituted by 'I') the situation of the 'I' pole is analogous to a kind of complex tug-of-war. We must imagine countless teams all of whose ropes are knotted at a centre; of differing strength, some directly combining, others obliquely affecting, many diametrically opposed. This central knot is the 'I'; and the diverse forces pulling at it make the state of tension.

TENSION

16 Tension is the effect on the individual of conflicting feelings, ideas, desires and events. Sometimes the tug-of-war will be one-sided, in the sense that the individual will know quite clearly which 'side' he wishes to win. In most political and social contexts this is so. A Jew-hater is not attracted by pro-semitism, a pacifist by armed intervention. There is still tension, since the individual knows that in society the opposing point of view is held. But in many other situations the conflict will be in the individual. He will be pulled first one way, then the other. This can form a rhythmic and comfortable pattern, as in normal sexual relationships; it can become a torture on the rack; and in extreme cases the knotted ropes, the individual mind, may break under the strain.

17 The effect of a tension may be good or bad: a game or an anxiety. Tension, like every other mechanism in the universal process, is indifferent to the organisms it affects. It may ravish them, or it may destroy them.

18 Each of us, and each society, and each world, is the centre of a web of such tensions; and what we call

progress is simply the effect of its opposing forces. To be human, or to be a human institution, is like being obliged to be a man on a tightrope. He must balance; and he must move.

19 We shall never attain a state of perfect balance. For us, the only perfect balance can be the living balance. Even if perfect balance is momentarily achieved, time ensures it will not be sustained. It is time that makes this balancing real.

20 Evolution changes in order to remain the same; but we change in order to become different. Time passes, from our human point of view, in order that each moment shall be in hazard and needing balance.

21 Our pleasure and our pain, our happiness and our envy, tell us each hour whether we balance or we fall. We live in the best of all possible worlds for mankind because we have been so adapted and developed that this world cannot be anything else to us; we are best and happiest in a tensional, tightrope situation, but one in which we can gain increasing skill as we go higher. Height in this situation is principally definable by our ability to destroy ourselves. The higher we go, the steadier—and what is steadiness if not a form of equality?—we must become. Or we fall.

THE MECHANISM OF THE TENSION

22 The fundamental tension is between pleasure and pain; and the three chief fields in which pleasure-pain operates are in the subsidiary tensions formed by good-evil, beauty-ugliness and security-insecurity. The

fundamental truth about all these tensions is that their 'good' poles are totally dependent for their 'goodness' —their value to us—on their 'bad' counterpoles. We all know this: that too much beauty can become ugliness, pain can become a profound pleasure . . . and so with all the rest.

23   Beauty-ugliness may serve as a model for the mechanism of the other tensions. Just as there are two modes of pleasure, intended and fortuitous, so are there two similar modes in our apprehension of beauty: *objective* and *actual*. The *objective* beauty of an object or experience is immutable, in parenthesis from all the subjective reactions and feelings of the experiencer. The *actual* beauty is what I happen to feel on a given occasion; it is the effect of the object or experience on my being *at that moment*.

24   We are taught as children to think about great art (and indeed many other things, such as religion) in the objective way, as if every actual experience of a great painting should produce the same effect on us. We see the results of this in any famous art gallery during the holiday season: the gaping, wooden-faced crowds who stare at great art and cannot understand why they are not having great-art reactions, because they have been so conditioned that they cannot accept that in *actuality* a Coca-Cola advertisement *may* be more beautiful than the sublimest Michelangelo.

25   Objective beauty is, of course, a myth—a very convenient myth, without which education in art and the 'science' of artistic appreciation would be impossible, and also a very human myth, since to search for the objective beauty in an object is to attempt to see it with the finer feelings of one's fellow-men. All great

works of art are secular ikons; and seeing them objectively is a secular act of communion.

26 But the objective beauty has two great enemies: reality and familiarity. The total reality of an aesthetic experience is what we actually feel both in and out of the parenthesis. Familiarity breeds contempt, that is, boredom with the parenthesis. Seeing the objective beauty becomes a duty, and we all know that the concepts of duty and pleasure are rarely sympathetic; the second visit to a gallery is also a visit to the first visit. This is not to say that all repetitions of beautiful experiences diminish the original beauty. It is often not true of art, and is certainly not generally true of many other activities—such as lovemaking. Nonetheless, there is a deep and archetypal hatred of routine in man, caused by the demands of survival (survival is the correct performance of drills, whether they be the hunting-planting drills of primitive man or the wage-seeking labour drills of industrial man). Pleasure is associated strongly with the unexpected (the fortuitous mode) and the fresh, or previously unexperienced, beauty.

27 It is of course possible to experience this beauty, which I will call *virgin,* in familiar objects, just as a metaphorical virginity can be found in a lover long after the literal virginity has passed. Such virgin beauty is commonly felt by almost all children, by poets and artists, and sometimes as an effect of certain drugs, like alcohol and lysergic acid. But to the vast majority of adults it can be found only in the new experience.

28 It is true that we find substitutes for the loss of the virgin beauty of an object. This picture is beautiful because it is mine; because I own it, or remember it, or understand its secrets. The thing becomes my

thing; not the thing in itself. Experience cedes to possession.

29 The whole trend of modern society is to force the objective beauty down our throats. It is this beauty that concerns critics; and we are an age of critics. It is this beauty that concerns commerce. Mass communications, vulgarizing techniques, the substitution of twentieth-century didactic culture for nineteenth-century didactic morality as a proof that the propagating organ 'serves' the public, the spread of museums and art galleries, the flood of books of information—all these things force us, fundamentally actual beings, to see the world in a parenthetically objective way.

30 The great contemporary attraction of the drugs and philosophies—such as Zen Buddhism—that facilitate the discovery of virgin beauty in familiar objects is explicable by our resentment of this pressure modern society puts on us. There are genuine and important uses for the objective beauty; but sometimes we want less of names, less of labels, less of analysis and historical placing—in a word, less 'culture'. We want nothing to stand between the object or experience now and the mind and senses now. We want the thing in itself.

31 In wanting this, and in being forced to search for the previously unexperienced, we put ourselves in the same situation as Midas. Everything he touched turned to gold, and from then on became useless to him. We crave the virgin beauty, but as soon as we experience it, it turns to gold . . . or boredom. We have to move on. The satisfaction of the desire is the creation of a new desire.

32 But there is of course a further element in our pursuit

of the virgin experience of beauty. Even the most un-observant must have noticed that the same inexorable law applies here as applies with hunger: the evil or apparently hostile state is necessary for our enjoy-ment of the good or 'friendly' one.

33   *Hunger and appetite are exactly the same thing.* Have you got an appetite? Yes, I am hungry. Are you hungry? Yes, I have an appetite.

34   The same is true of all the other great tensions. A pleasure is all the more pleasurable for coming after a period of pain. Security, for following insecurity. Good, for following evil. It is true that we may not actively seek the 'bad' counterpoles and our swing away from the 'good' ones may be characterized more by apathy than by actually inflicting pain on our-selves, or risking our lives meaninglessly, or engaging in crime. Nevertheless we cannot do without the alter-nation of these opposed states, and we will encourage the alternation to the extent that we feel deprived, by the defects of society and education, by the unneces-sary inequality in our world, of the virgin experiences we need.

35   In our present unhappy stage of civilization—come so far, so little learned—it is natural that many should regard the essential thing to be the virgin experience, whether it occurs among the socially 'good' or 'bad' poles. They will find a justification for crime (a case brilliantly put by Jean Genet), for non-criminal evil (persistent adultery, ruthless commercial practice and so on) and for insecurity (the pursuit of dangerous interests and professions, such as mountaineering and car-racing).

36   Even those who try to find their pleasures in the

'good' poles will just as much need, even if they do not actively seek experience in, the 'bad' poles.

37 Now it may seem at first sight that this alternating mechanism reaches so deep into our innermost beings, and into the innermost being of our societies, that we can do nothing about it. But this is to say that reason and science can do nothing against the pleasure principle and our addiction to the virgin experience; that we can never control the violent effects that these tensions at present exert on each of us and the societies we live in. I reject totally this pessimistic and fatalistic view of human destiny, and I want to suggest the model and method we should examine for a solution.

THE MANIPULATION OF THE TENSIONS

38 The model is marriage; the method is transposition; and what we hope to achieve is not of course the abolition of all tension, but the avoidance of wasted energy, pointless battle and unnecessary suffering. It is necessary to drink water; but it should not be necessary to drink polluted water.

39 Joining is a first principle; the proton joins the electron, the atoms by joining grow in complicacy, make molecules by joining, amoeba joins amoeba, male joins female, mind mind, country country: existence is being joined. Being is joining, and the higher the being the more the joining.

40 Marriage is the best general analogy of existing. It is the most familiar polar situation, with the most familiar tension; and the very fact that reproduction re-

quires a polar situation is an important biological explanation of why we think polarly.

41   As with all tensional states, marriage is harassed by a myth and a reality. The objective myth is that of the Perfect Marriage, a supposedly achievable state of absolute harmony between the partners. The reality is whatever is the case, every actual marriage.

42   Married couples normally try to give the public, their friends, and even their children, a Perfect Marriage version of their own marriage; if they do not, then they still express and judge the extent of their failure by the standards of the Perfect Marriage.

43   The gauges of the supposedly Perfect Marriage are passion and harmony. But passion and harmony are antipathetic. A marriage may begin in passion and end in harmony, but it cannot be passionate and harmonious at the same time.

44   Passion is a pole, an extreme joining; it can only be achieved as height is on a swing—by going from coital pole to sundered counterpole; from two to two ones. The price of passion is no passion.

45   During the White Terror, the police caught two suspects, a man and a woman, who were passionately in love. The chief of police invented a new torture. He simply had them bound as one, face to face. To begin with, the lovers consoled themselves that at least they were together, even though it was with the inseparability of Siamese twins. But slowly each became irksome to the other; they became filthy, they could not sleep; and then hateful; and finally so intolerably loathsome that when they were released they never spoke to each other again.

46 A few rare marriages may be without mutual hatred or quarrels from their very beginning. One could also write music in which every interval was of a perfect fourth. But it would not be perfect music. Most marriages recognize this paradox: that passion destroys passion, as the Midas touch destroys possession.

47 An intelligent married couple might therefore come to this conclusion: they wish to retain passion in their marriage, and so they should deliberately quarrel, and hate, in order to swing back together with more force. Women do indeed initiate marital quarrels more frequently than men; they know more about human nature, more about mystery, and more about keeping passion alive. There may be biological reasons for menstruation, but it is also the most effective recreator of passion; and the women who resist emancipation also know what they are about.

48 But there comes a time when passion costs too much in quarrels. To survive familiarity, dailiness, it needs more and more violent separations, and so either the two poles quarrel more and more violently inside marriage, or they look for new passion, a new pole, outside it.

49 Passion can be controlled in only one way; by sacrificing its pleasures.

50 But this sacrifice is made almost impossibly difficult, at least in capitalist Western society, by our attitude to growing old. With the decline of a belief in an afterlife and the corresponding growth of the demand for equality, the whole tendency of man is to shrink away from death and the age at which it arrives. In every aspect of our societies, from their art to their advertising, we see the cult and desirability of eternal

youth maintained . . . and therefore of passion, which joined with our craving for the virgin experience, explains the enormous change that has taken place in our concepts and standards of marital fidelity.

51 Man is more guilty than woman here, since men have always required public and social—rather than emotional and domestic—reward in life. In spite of the male myth about female vanity, it is the men who are in the more greedy pursuit of this chimera of eternal youth. The Western male has, in our century, become increasingly Moslem in his attitude towards marriage and women. We do not yet practice legal polygamy, but the common contemporary desire of men in their forties and fifties to jettison their similarly-aged wives for an affaire or a new marriage with a girl young enough to be a daughter (or even a grand-daughter) is already a *de facto* polygamous institution among the rich and successful in the less convention-bound professions (especially those that permit mobility and thus escape the ethical pressures of the close community). This may be a normal, even finally a healthy, innovation in society. But it could be *just* only if middle-aged women were allowed to follow suit. In fact, they stay at home and suffer, left in a slavery more subtle but no less iron than the one they are generally supposed to have been freed from during these last fifty years.

52 This retrogressive step in the relationship between the sexes is certainly partly explicable as a last resentment of overthrown Adam against victorious Eve; and it may in itself seem to have little to do with my general theme. But it is in fact very symptomatic of our craving for a more sharply-opposed tonality of life—a greater tension. No one will deny that passion is necessary in its season, and we possess nothing

until we possess it first with passion. But this passion, and the passionate stage of marriage, is animal; it is the harmonius marriage that is human. In passion, it is said, we feel near the heart of things—and so we are: nearer things than humanity.

53 Plenty of books instruct sexual technique; but none teach the equally vital technique of transposing from the passionate relationship to the harmonious one.

TRANSPOSITION

54 The first step is to eliminate passion as a source of tension. The second is to accept the oneness of the marriage. In passion everything is between thee and me; in harmony it is between them and us. I-thou is passion, we-they is harmony. We have the word ego-centric; it is time we invented *noscentric.*

55 Now of course no marriage can be wholly harmonious. But if it becomes noscentric it is immediately equipped to find different counterpoles, outside itself, which can in their turn help to determine the nature of, and establish and cement, the *nos,* the 'we' pole; just as the 'I' pole is determined by its counterpoles. Certain counterpoles, such as the problems of aging, and the approach of death, will be common to all marriages.

56 But there is a second aid to the establishment of the harmonious marriage. We think ordinarily of the opposite of harmony as discord. But as I said earlier there is another and very fundamental counterpole of every existent object, and that is its non-existence—nothingness, the state of 'God'. In a piece of music we think of the discords as the counterpoles of the harmonies; but there are also the pauses and silences.

And it is this state, not of discord but of 'silent' not-harmony, that we need to utilize to establish the harmonious marriage. In practical terms, this means the establishment of private interests not shared by the other partner, a disconnection in the relationship, an acceptance that togetherness becomes as intolerable as that of the pair in the White Terror torture if it is not based on periods of at least psychological separation. Now clearly the ability to form such outside interests, to maintain such a controlled separateness from which the basic harmony will spring, requires both education and economic freedom of a standard we have nowhere in our world today except among the fortunate few; and that is yet one more argument for a greater human equality.

57   All I say about marriage is stale news: every middle-aged and still happily married couple knows it. But my purpose is to point out that *in our metaphorical marriage to pleasure, and in particular to the pleasures of being secure, doing good, and experiencing beauty, we develop the same kind of passionate relationship as we do in marriage.* We feel passionately about them, but in order to continue to feel so, we have increasingly to resort to their counterpoles.

58   The equivalent in marriage is the malaise known as the seven-year-itch: boredom with fidelity. This metaphorical itch, this boredom with the stable and the socially recommended and the good, comes as a rule between the ages of thirty and forty—in the fourth decade of the marriage to existence. It is aggravated —and always will be—by the group in society who are at the age when the passionate experience is their right, their desire, and almost their duty: that is, the young. And if we idolize (as we do today) the young, then passionate atmospheres (and passionate politics,

passionate art, and all the rest) *must* infest our societies.

INTERNATIONAL TENSION

59 All this conflict between harmony and passion becomes of greatest pertinence in the relationship between different countries and blocs of countries. The suffering we cause by private stupidity is at least confined to a small area; but the penalties now lurking in the underground bunkers and germ-warfare laboratories, lurking and waiting to pounce on any national or governmental selfishness and stupidity, are so gigantic that we cannot afford any personal isolationism in these matters.

60 Countries and blocs also live in relationships like marriage. To have the passion of love (to live in peace, which in the world as it is means in a state where the over-privileged are left in safe possession of their privileges) they have to have war. So ages of prosperity and security breed the counterpoles. An age of self is always mother to an age of war.

61 It is customary to talk of 'international tension' and 'nuclear annihilation' as if these things were terrible. But we love the terror. It is like salt to us. We live under the threat of an annihilatory war; and on it.

62 The two world wars were wars among societies dominated by the emotions of the adolescent. East and West, unhappily and passionately married in the house of the world, both derive vigour and energy from their mutual love-hatred. They erect and exercise and thrill each other. They stimulate each other in many ways besides the economic.

63 There are enough hostile factors (overpopulation,

poverty, disease, ignorance) in the human situation to provide endless extramarital counterpoles. There is no inescapable need for man to be his own worst enemy. Many other things are queueing close to have that role.

THE ULTIMATE TENSION

64   The power of a tension is proportionate to its mystery. To be aware of and to understand a tension produces two results. Like lightning on a dark night it reveals what is, and it reveals the way ahead. It thus allows the transposition to a personally or socially less harmful tension to be made. It permits the tension to be controlled, rather than to control.

65   Knowledge of a tension therefore inaugurates two situations: a seeing through the old, and a craving for a new. Because we love and need mystery, we are often reluctant to analyze situations in which mystery seems to inhere. The chief such situation is in ourselves, in the tensions we exist in. We despise primitive cultures for the taboos with which they surround sacred groves and caves and the like; but we still encourage exactly similar taboos in the antique landscapes of the mind.

66   Yet even here we must distinguish between the selfish attachment to mystery that is really a lazy refusal to think or act and our essential need of a residual mystery in life as a whole. This mystery, between what we know and what we know we will never know, is the ultimate tension.

67   The more knowledge we have the more intense this mystery becomes. It may diminish from our point of view, but it condenses.

68 We tend to think that evolution must be a vast attack on mystery. We suppose our highest goal must be to know all. We consequently try to ignore, or destroy, or vitiate, what genuine mysteries life contains.

69 We are intended to solve much of the mystery; it is harmful to us. We have to invent protections against the sun, in many situations; but to wish to destroy the sun? The easier mysteries, how at a superficial level things work mechanically, how things are 'caused', have been largely solved. Many take these mysteries for the whole mystery. The price of tapping water into every house is that no one values water any more.

70 The task of education is to show the mysteries solved; but also to show where mystery has not been, and will not be, solved—and in the most familiar objects and events. There is mystery enough at noon; no need to multiply the midnight rites.

71 The counterpole of all that is existent and known or knowable, that is 'God', must be infinite mystery, since only so can a tension remain to keep mankind from collapsing into total knowledge, or a 'perfect' world that would be a perfect hell. From this knowledge-mystery tension there is no transposing; and it is the source of human being.

72 All predictions are wagers. All predictions about the future are about what is not scientifically certain, but only scientifically probable. This fundamental uncertainty is essential to life. Every look forward is a potential illusion. This satisfies our need for insecurity; since in an eternally insecure situation we must externally seek knowledge and security, and never completely find them.

7

OTHER PHILOSOPHIES

1 We may reject some of these as we might reject certain houses to live in; we cannot reject them as houses for anyone else to live in, we cannot deny them utility in part, beauty in part, meaningfulness in part; and therefore truth in part.

2 Ernst Mach: *A piece of knowledge is never false or true—but only more or less biologically and evolutionally useful.* All dogmatic creeds are approximations: these approximations form a humus from which better approximations grow.*

CHRISTIANITY

3 In a hundred years ecclesiastical Christianity will be dead. It is already a badly-flawed utility. The current ecumenical mania, the 'glorious new brotherhood' of churches, is a futile scrabbling behind the wainscots of reality.

4 This is not to deny what Christianity has done for humanity. It was instituted by a man of such active philosophical and evolutionary genius that it is little wonder that he was immediately called (as it was a necessary part of his historical efficacy that he should be) divine.

5 Christianity has protected the most precarious, because most evolved, section of the human race from

102

itself. But in order to sell its often sound evolutionary principles it was obliged to 'lie'; and these 'lies' made it temporarily more, but now finally less, effective.

6 In no foreseeable future will many of the general social laws and attitudes stated or implied in Christianity be archaic; this is because they are based on compassion and common sense. But there is in every great religion a process akin to the launching of space vehicles; an element that gives the initial boost, the getting off the ground, and an element that stays aloft. Those who cling to Christian metaphysical dogma are trying to keep launcher and launched together.

7 Furthermore, the essential appeal of a religion will always be racial, and always more accessible to the originating race or racial group than to others. A religion is a specific reaction to an environment, a historical predicament; and therefore always in some sense inadequate to those who live in different environments and predicaments.

8 First the buttress of dogmatic faith strengthens, then it petrifies; just as the heavy armour of some prehistoric reptiles first enabled them to survive and then caused them to disappear. A dogma is a form of reaction to a special situation; it is never an adequate reaction to all situations.

9 The Bet Situation: however much evidence of historical probability the theologians produce for the incredible (in terms of modern scientific credibility) events of the life of Jesus, they can never show that these events took place verifiably in the way they claim they took place. The same is finally true, of course, of any remote historical event. We are always reduced, in

the bitter logical end, to the taking of some such decision as the Kierkegaardian step in the dark of the
Pascalian *pari;* and if I refuse to believe these incredible events took place, then it can be said that I am
doing no more than taking my own blind step in the
opposite direction. A certain kind of blind believer,
not confined to Christianity but common in it since
the days of Tertullian, uses the apparent absurdity,
and the consequent despair, of our never being able
to establish any certainty of belief as both a source
of energy for the step in the dark and an indication of
the direction in which it should be taken. Because
(it is said) by any empirical human definition of what
constitutes knowing I cannot know anything finally,
I must leap to some state that does permit me to know
finally—a state of certainty 'above' or 'beyond' attain-
ment by empirical or rational means. But this is as if,
finding myself in doubt and in darkness, I should
decide, instead of cautiously feeling my way forward,
to leap; not only to leap, to leap desperately; and not
only to leap desperately, but into the darkest part of
the surrounding darkness. There is an obvious emotional heroic-defiant appeal about this violent plunge
from the battlements of reason; and an equally obvious lack of spiritual glamour in the cautious inching
forward by the dim light of probability and the inter-
mittent flicker (in this remote region) of scientific
method. But I believe, and my reason tells me I am
right to believe, that the step in the dark constitutes
an existential betrayal and blasphemy, which is the
maintaining that scientific probability should play no
part in matters of faith. On the contrary I believe
that probability must play a major part. I believe in
the situation and cosmos described in the first group
of notes here because it seems to me the most probable. No one but Jesus has been born of a virgin or
has risen on the third day, and these, like the other

incredible facts about him, are running at very long odds indeed. It is countless thousands of ,millions to one that I am right in refusing to believe in certain aspects of the Biblical accounts of his life, and countless thousands of millions to one that you, if you do believe them, are wrong.*

10 To take these incredible aspects from his life does not diminish Jesus; it enhances him. If Christians were to say that these incredible events and the doctrines and rituals evolved from them are to be understood metaphorically, I could become a Christian. I could believe in the Virgin Birth (that the whole of evolution, of whatever is the case, fathers each child); in the Resurrection (for Jesus has risen again in men's minds); in the Miracles (because we should all like to perform such generous acts); in the Divinity of Christ and in Transubstantiation (we are all complementary one to another, and all to 'God'); I could believe in all these things that at present excommunicate my reason. But traditional Christians would call this lack of faith.

11 Intelligent Athenians of the fifth century knew their gods were metaphors, personifications of forces and principles. There are many signs that the athenianization of Christianity has begun. The second coming of Christ will be the realization that Jesus of Nazareth was supremely human, not supremely divine; but this will be to relegate him to the ranks of the philosophers and to reduce the vast apparatus of ritual, church and priesthood to an empty shell.

12 It is not what Jesus made of mankind, but what mankind made of him.

13 The Christian churches, contrary to the philosophy of

Jesus himself, have frequently made their own self-continuance their chief pre-occupation. They have fostered poverty, or indifference to it; they have forced people to look beyond life; they have abused the childish concept of hell and hell-fire; they have supported reactionary temporal powers; they have condemned countless innocent pleasures and bred centuries of bigotry; they have set themselves up as refuges and too often taken good care that outside their doors refuge shall be needed. Things are better now; but we have not forgotten that things were not better till history presented the churches with a clear choice: reform or die.

14 A similar scramble to clean up the house is taking place today in Christian theology; but it comes too late. There are 'advanced' Christian thinkers who propose a god not very different from the one I have described earlier. They wish to humanize Jesus, to demythologize the Bible, to turn Christianity into something bizarrely like an early Marxism. Everything we once understood to be Christianity is now, we are told, a metaphor of a deeper truth. But if we can now see this deeper truth, then the metaphor is unnecessary. The new theologians are sawing the branches they sit on; and they are bound to fall.

15 Worst of all, the churches have jealously caged Jesus. What right have they to say that he cannot be approached except through them? Must I believe in the Olympians and practise ancient Greek religious rituals before I can approach Socrates? The church has become not the body and spirit of Jesus; but a screen and barrier round him.

16 Jesus was human. Perhaps he believed he was all that he claimed to be; but that he was not all that he

claimed to be is trivial, not vital, because he was human; and because the essence of his teaching does not depend on his divinity.

17 There is no redemption, no remission; a sin has no price. It cannot be bought back till time itself is bought back.

18 Children learn very early the double vision a dogmatic church induces. They pray to God and nothing happens. They learn that there are two modes of behaviour, an absolute one in church, and a relative one outside. They are taught science and then ordered to believe what is palpably unscientific. They are told to revere the Bible, and yet even they can see that it is in one way a rag bag of myths, tribal gibberish, wild vindictiveness, insane puritanism, garbled history, absurdly one-sided propaganda—and in another way a monument of splendid poetry, profound wisdom, crowned by the richly human story of Jesus.

19 It is not the child adopting double standards who is to blame; it is the churches that perpetuate them. To claim of something that it belongs to a special category of·absolute truth or reality is to pronounce its death sentence: there is no absolute truth or reality.

20 After Platonism, and surrounded by the puerilities of the debased classical religion of the later Roman civilization, Mediterranean man was bound to develop a monotheistic and ethically-inclined counter-religion. A kind of Jesus and a kind of Christianity was as inevitable as was a kind of Marx and Marxism in the later stages of the Industrial Revolution.

21 Humanity is like a tall building. It needs stage after

stage of scaffolding. Religion after religion, philosophy after philosophy; one cannot build the twentieth floor from the scaffolding of the first. The great religions prevent the Many from looking and thinking. The world would not at once be a happier place if they looked and they thought; but this is no defence of dogmatic religions.

22 Does one snatch a cripple's crutch away because it is not the latest sort? Is it even enough to put the latest sort in his hands? He may not know how to use it. But this is not an argument against the latest sort of crutch.

23 Religious faith: mystery. Rational faith: law. The fundamental nature of reality is mysterious—this is a *scientific* fact. In basing themselves on mystery, religions are more scientific than rational philosophies. But there are mysteries and mysteries; and Christianity has foolishly tried to particularize the fundamental mystery. The essential and only mystery is the nature of what the Christians call God or Providence. But the church has introduced a fairground of pseudo-mysteries, which have no relation to truth, but *only to the truth that mystery has power.*

24 Yet man is starved of mystery: so starved that even the most futile enigmas have their power still. If no one will write new detective stories, then people will still read the old ones. Virgin birth makes Jesus unique; the mystery of this impudent uniqueness is so pleasurable that we cannot resist it.

25 In most parts of the world the horse and cart has been superseded by the automobile. But we do not say of the horse and cart that it is untrue, or that simply because the automobile is generally more use-

ful and faster all horses and carts should be abolished. There are still places where the horse and cart is indispensable. Where it is used and useful it is evolutionally true.

26   Militant anti-religious movements are based on this mechanization fallacy: that the most efficient machine must be the best. But it is the most effective machine in the circumstances that is the best.

27   If the necessity of the situation is that it should be softened, misted, muffled, then Christianity is good. There are many such situations. If to a man dying of cancer Christianity makes dying of cancer an easier death, not all the arguments of all the anti-Christians could make me believe Christianity, *in this situation,* is not true. But this truth is a kind of utility, and in general I think it probable that clear glass is of greater utility than frosted.

28   For every Christian who believes in all the dogma of his church, there are a thousand who half believe because they feel a man should believe in something. If the old religions survive, it is because they are convenient receptacles of the desire to believe; and because they are, though poor ones, ports; and because they at least try to satisfy the hunger for mystery.

29   All the old religions cause a barbarous waste of moral energy; ramshackle water mills on a river that could serve hydro-electric dynamos.

30   All gods alleged to be capable of intervention in our existence are idols; all images of gods are idols; all prayer to them, all adoration of them, is idolatry.

31   Gratitude for having been born and for existing is an

archetypal human feeling; so is gratitude for good
health, good fortune and happiness. But such gratitude should be ploughed back into the life around
one, into one's *manner* of being; not thrown vaguely
into the sky or poured into that most odious of concealed narcissisms, prayer. Religion stands between
people's gratitude and the practical uses they might
put its energy to. One good work is worth more than
a million good words; and this would be true even if
there were an observing and good-mark-awarding
god 'above' us.

32 I reject Christianity, along with the other great religions. Most of its mysteries are remote from the true
mystery. Though I admire the founder, though I
admire many priests and many Christians, I despise
the church. It is because men want to be good and do
good that it has survived so long; like Communism, it
is inherently parasitical on a deeper and more mysterious nobility in man than any existing religion
or political creed can satisfy.

LAMAISM

33 Life is pain, suffering, betrayal, catastrophe, and even
its pleasures are delusions; the wise man teaches himself to empty his mind of all that is mere triviality,
futile flux, and thus learns to live in a state of mys-
tical inward peace. Man is brought into the world in
order that he may, by *ascesis,* train himself to withdraw from it, and thus, it is claimed, transcend it.
So the lama refuses to participate in society; it is by
extirpating his animal desires and his vain life in society that demonstrates true freedom. He does not
resist the nemo; he invites it.

34 Recent world history has driven many in all the con-
tinents into this view of life. Few can withdraw totally from their society. But there is a secular lamaism
that is widespread. These semi-lamas can be identified
as follows: they refuse to commit themselves in any
meaningful way on any social or political or metaphysical questions, and not because of genuine scepticism, but because of indifference to society and all
that is connected with it.

35 A semi-lama is one who thinks that to ask nothing of
his fellow men permits him to insist that nothing shall
be asked of him; as if, in the human context, to contract no debts is to owe nothing. But we all drift on
the same raft. There is only one question. What sort
of shipwrecked man shall I be?

36 Freedom of will can be increased only by exercise.
But the only place where such exercise can be got is
in society; and to opt out of that is to opt out of
opting. If I jump off a high building I prove I can
jump; but I am the one who most needs the proof.
The proof is meaningless if I cannot apply it. Why
prove Pythagoras to a corpse?

37 The lama allows his desire to be free of society to
dupe him into thinking he is indeed free. He no
longer sees the prison walls. Nothing will make him
believe they exist.

38 There is in oriental lamaism an acute apprehension
of the nature of 'God'. But the mistake is to use this
apprehension as a model for humans to copy. Lamaism tells us to make a sustained attempt to achieve
oneness with 'God', or nothingness. Living, I must
learn not to be, or to be as if I was not; individual, I
must lose all individuality; I must totally withdraw

from all life and yet be in total sympathy with all life. But if we were all lamas it would be as if we were all masturbators: life would end. 'God' is in contrast to us; it is our pole. And it is not by imitating it, as the Tao Te Ching recommends, that we honour it; nor does it need honouring.

39 The semi-lama is usually a sensitive person who finds himself frustrated and horrified by the futility and ugliness of life around him. His lamasery is commonly art, which he loves and regards in a characteristically narcissistic and barren way. He enjoys form rather than content; style rather than meaning; vogue rather than social significance; fastidiousness rather than strength. He will often get more pleasure from the minor arts than the major ones, and more pleasure from minor works of art than from major ones. He becomes a connoisseur, a collector, a hypersensitive critic. A taster, a tongue, a palate, or an eye, an ear; and all the rest of his humanity becomes atrophied and drops away.

40 It is true that lamaism, especially in such forms as Zen Buddhism, has a great deal to tell us about the enjoyment of objects as objects; about the beauty of the leaf and the beauty of the leaf in the wind. But this perfecting of the aesthetic sense and this clarifying of the inner metaphor in each, cannot be taken as a way of life. It may be, almost certainly is, a constituent of the good life; but it is not the good life.

41 Lamaism, the withdrawal into self-preoccupation or self-enjoyment, is the perennial philosophy; that is, the philosophy against which all others (like Christianty) are erected. To the extent that we have to nourish self in order to remain healthy psychologically it is as important as the food we eat. But clearly it

will flourish most when the self, or individual, feels
most defeated and most in danger. The most frequent
argument in defence of it then is that someone must
guard and preserve the highest standards of living.
In the lives of even the most selfish castes and élites
there is something good *in itself;* but this is surely the
most relative goodness of all. Early Sèvres porcelain
is beautiful; but it was not made only of clay, it was
made also of the emaciated flesh and bones of every
French peasant who starved during the period of its
making. All the luxuries we buy ourselves are paid
for in the same coin; no economic or cultural plea is
sound in the final analysis. Under all its names—
hedonism, epicureanism, 'beat' philosophy—lamaism
is a resource of the defeated. There might be worlds
and systems of existence where it was tenable; but
not in one like ours, in a permanent state of evolutionary war.

HUMANISM

42   Humanism is a philosophy of the law, of what can be
rationally established. It has two great faults. One lies
in its inherent contempt for the mysterious, the irrational and the emotional. The other is that humanism
is of its nature tolerant: but tolerance is the observer's virtue, not the governor's.

43   The characteristic movement of the humanist is to
withdraw; to live on the Sabine farm; to write *Odi
profanum vulgus, et arceo.* A humanist is someone
who sees good in his enemies and good in their philosophies; he sees good in his enemies because he
cannot accept that they are freely evil, and he sees
good in their philosophies because no philosophy is
without some reason and some humanity. He lives by

the golden mean, by reason, by the middle of the
road, by seeing both sides; he captures respect, but
not the imagination.*

44 It is conventionally held that ancient polytheistic
humanism collapsed because it was unrealistic, a
highly artificial system. But there is a sense in which
it was realistic, as we should expect in any religion
springing from Greek origins. The gods on Olympus
at least represented *actual* human attributes, or varying and often conflicting archetypal human tendencies; while the Hebraic system—the uniting of
desirable (moralistic) human attributes into *one* god
—was a highly artificial procedure. In many ways the
Greek system is the more rational and intelligent;
which perhaps explains why it has been the less ap-
pealing. The Hebrew god is a creation of man; and
the Greek gods are a reflection of him.

45 We often forget to what an extent the Renaissance,
and all its achievements, sprang from a reversion to
the Greek system. The relationship between pagan-
ism and freedom of thought is too well established to
need proof; and all monotheistic religions are in a
sense puritan in tone—inherently tyrannical and
fascistic. The great scientific triumphs of the Greeks,
their logic, their democracy, their arts, all were made
possible by their loose, fluid concepts of divinity; and
the same is true of the most recent hundred years of
human history.

46 But the opposition is not, of course, simply between
a 'liberal' polytheism and an 'illiberal' monotheism.
Religion has always been for man intensely a field of
self-interest; and it is plainly harder to bargain with,
or blindly believe in, several gods than one. A certain
scepticism and agnosticism, so characteristic of the

best Greek thought, is a natural product of polytheism; just as emotional enthusiasm and mystic
fervour breed from its opposite. This conflict between
scepticism and mysticism long pre-dates the Christian era.

47 Like modern humanists, the ancient Milesians did
not believe in an afterlife or in any god. Then, in the
seventh and eighth centuries before Christ, came the
Orphic revivalist invasion with its Irish stew of redemption, salvation and predestined grace, and all
the power of its wild mysteries. By the fifth century
the battle between Orphic mysticism and Milesian
scepticism was permanent. There has never been
peace since between Dionysus and Apollo, and there
never will be.*

48 Nonetheless, periods of history come when it seems
clear which serves the general need best. Monotheism
saw man through the dark ages that followed the
collapse of the Roman empire; but today the benevolent scepticism of humanism seems better suited to
our situation. What is evident is that it is ridiculous
to regard this opposition as a struggle or battle, in
which one side must be defeated and the other victorious; instead it should be regarded as the nature of
the human polity, the *sine qua non* of being in society
and in evolution.

49 A Christian says: 'If all were good, all would be
happy'. A socialist says: 'If all were happy, all would
be good'. A fascist says: 'If all obeyed the state, all
would be both happy and good'. A lama says: 'If all
were like me, happiness and goodness would not
matter'. A humanist says: 'Happiness and goodness
need more analysis'. This last is the least deniable
view.

SOCIALISM

50 Napoleon once said: 'Society cannot exist without inequality of wealth, and inequality of wealth cannot exist without religion'. He was not of course speaking as a theorist of history, but justifying his Concordat with the Vatican; however, this Machiavellian statement suggests admirably both the aims and the difficulties of socialism.

51 Socialism-Communism is an attempt to readjust and to reinterpret Christianity. But among the features of Christianity it sent to the guillotine was the essential one: mystery. Christianity rots because it attempts to preserve a false mystery; socialism will rot because it attempts to abolish a true one.

52 Like Christianity, it has retained the launching mechanism too long after the launching. In order to achieve a greater social justice, the early socialists disseminated various striking but crude theories of equality, of materialism, of history; they idolized the proletariat and blackened all that was not the proletariat. They turned socialism into a bludgeon, a vast explosion. What we need now is not a vast explosion. We need less force, and more thought; less doctrine, and more assessment.

53 For all its hostility to earlier religions, socialism is a religion itself; and this is nowhere more apparent than in its hatred of heresy, of any criticism that does not take certain articles of dogma as incontrovertible statements about reality. Acceptance of dogma becomes a chief proof of one's faith in the creed. This leads at once to petrifaction.

54   The great problem at the heart of socialism is this: in order to bring social justice to the many, the leaders of socialism were obliged to give them power. But the proletariat are far more skilled at discovering what they want than what they need; so giving them power constituted giving them power to say what they want, not giving them objectivity to see what they need. What the many need above all else is education; they need to be led, not to be leaders. It is this delicate balance that socialist leaders have to keep—on one hand to stay in power they must placate the desires of the many for consumer goods, for the tawdry trivia of life, sufficiently to ensure that they shall not be outbid by the right wing (and even in the most Communist countries there is a right wing), and on the other hand they have to persuade the many that there are nobler things in life than unrestrained free enterprise and the pursuit of cream cake and television circuses. They need the power, the might of the people, and then the consent of the people to the proposition that might is not right; that a universal and ill-educated electorate needs guidance as well as obedience from its elected representatives and governors.

55   Socialism has its afterlife myth, not in a hypothetical other world, but in a hypothetical future of this world. Marxism and Leninism both proclaim, use and abuse the notion of perfectibility; justifying bad means by good ends.

56   Socialism has other myths, such as that of the intrinsic nobility of labour. *But it is not the capitalist who ultimately exploits the worker; it is the work itself.*

57   The welfare state provides material welfare and

psychological illfare. Too much social security and equality breed individual restlessness and frustration: hazard starvation and variety starvation. The nightmare of the welfare state is boredom.

58 Full employment, a planned economy, state ownership of primary industries, national insurance and free medical treatment are admirable things in a society. But such provisions require other provisions. We fortify one flank, and trust the enemy not to attack the other. But evolution knows no chivalry. The higher the standard of living, the greater the need for variety. The greater the leisure, the greater the lack of tension. And the price of salt rises.

59 The welfare state as at present envisaged annihilates factors that evolution values highly: hazard and mystery. This is not an argument against the general principle of the welfare state, but against the inadequacy of present notions of the welfare state, and of what constitutes equality. We need less *egalité,* and more *fraternité.*

60 Social stagnation is most likely to occur in extreme societies—extremely just or extremely unjust—and must lead to one of three things: war, decay, or revolution.

61 We need a science that studies the amount of variety, of excitement, of change, of risk of all kinds that the average individual and the average society needs; and why they should need them.

62 Socialism is bedevilled by the spirit of endless and unconsidered yearning towards an impossible equality, conservatism by the pig belief that the fortunate must at all costs ensure their good fortune. Christianity and

socialism have both partly failed. In the no-man's-land between the two stagnant armies there is only one philosophy: the conservative one of self.

63 Yet both Christianity and socialism gain adherents, simply because they are both fighting against a worse creed; and because they appear to be the best public utilizers of right private belief. But they are like armaments manufacturers. Their health is dependent on the continuance of the battle in which they are engaged, and therefore, paradoxically, on the very aims they profess publicly to oppose. Where there is poverty and social injustice, both Christianity and Communism may flourish.

64 Communism and socialism strengthen capitalism and Christianity, and vice versa. Both sides dream of the total extermination of the other; but in the now they need each other, and counter-support each other.

65 In a world in which many societies and racial blocs are on the verge of growing so large that they will have to exterminate one another to survive, and in which the means rapidly to effect such an extermination are at hand, conservatism, the philosophy of unrestricted free enterprise, of self, of preserving the *status quo,* is obviously the wrong and dangerous one. If conservatism, the right wing, has so much power and influence in the so-called 'free' world today it is because autocratic doctrinaire socialism of the Communist kind seems a worse alternative. If humans have to choose between an unfair free society and a fair unfree one, they will always swing to the first alternative, because freedom is man's magnetic north. There is thus more hope for mankind in parliamentary socialism of the kind evolved in Western Europe than in any other political tendency; and

this is in spite of the doctrinaire and other weaknesses I have suggested earlier.

66 Above all, socialism enshrines the vital concept that there is too much inequality in the world; and that this inequality can be remedied. The best socialism wishes to achieve a maximum of freedom with a minimum of social suffering. The intention is right, however wrong the means may sometimes be.

67 The task before parliamentary socialism is that of articulating and advocating its policies to an ill-educated electorate in a society where there is freedom to choose one's representatives; in short, where there is always the danger that the electorate will choose self rather than society. Where for electoral reasons its policies imitate conservatism, where it insists on measures for doctrinaire reasons, I reject socialism; and where its policies attack the fundamental freedom of choice of the electorate, as in Communism, I reject it. But when it expresses the desire of people freely able to choose other more self-advantageous policies to choose the inauguration of a juster world, I accept it. And how can men of good will support any other political creed?

FASCISM

68 Fascism maintains that it is the duty of the powerful and intelligent to gain control of the state so that the Many may be organized and controlled. At its Platonic best it is the most realistic of political philosophies. But it always breaks on the same rock: the individual.

69 It is the individual in us that makes us suspect meas-

ures of which we approve. We can always put ourselves in the place of those who disapprove. Individuality is a channel, a medium through which all individuals can communicate. It is a passport to all other individuals. But it is this essential intercommunicability of individualized intelligences that fascism sets out to destroy. Fascism and imagination are incompatible.

70 Fascists attempt to found a unipolar society. All must face south, none must face north. But in such societies there is a fatal attraction towards the counterpoles of whatever is commanded. If you *order* man to look to the future, he looks to the present. If you *order* him to worship God, he worships man. If you *order* him to serve the state, he serves himself.

71 Society needs some conformities, as a machine needs oil and rounded edges. But many societies demand conformity in precisely the matters where nonconformity is needed, and allow nonconformity where it should be banned. Nothing is more terrible in a society than this wastage or abuse of the desire to conform.

72 The good human society is one in which no one conforms without thinking why he is conforming; in which no one obeys without considering why he is obeying; and in which no one conforms out of fear or laziness. Such a society is not a fascist one.

EXISTENTIALISM

73 All states and societies are incipiently fascist. They strive to be unipolar, to make others conform. The true antidote to fascism is therefore existentialism; not socialism.

74 Existentialism is the revolt of the individual against all those systems of thought, theories of psychology, and social and political pressures that attempt to rob him of his individuality.

75 The best existentialism tries to re-establish in the individual a sense of his own uniqueness, a knowledge of the value of anxiety as an antidote to intellectual complacency (petrifaction), and a realization of the need he has to learn to choose and control his own life. Existentialism is then, among other things, an attempt to combat the ubiquitous and increasingly dangerous sense of the nemo in modern man.

76 Existentialism is inherently hostile to all organization of society and belief that does not permit the individual to choose, so often as he likes, to belong to it. This cussedness, this obstinate individualism, lays it open to misrepresentation by those *soi-disant* existentialists who are really anarchists or bohemians, and open to attack from those who hold the traditional views of social responsibility and the social contract.

77 There is an invitation in existentialism to reject traditional codes of morality and behaviour, especially when these are imposed by authority or society without any clear justification except that of tradition. There is a constant invitation to examine motives; the first existentialist was Socrates, not Kierkegaard. The Sartrean school invented commitment. But permanent commitment to religious or political dogma (so-called Catholic and Communist existentialism) is fundamentally unexistentialist; an existentialist has by his belief to judge every situation on its merits, to assess his motives anew before every situation, and

only then to choose. He never belongs as every organization wants its members to belong.

78 It is to me impossible to reject existentialism though it is possible to reject this or that existentialist action. Existentialism is not a philosophy, but a way of looking at, and utilizing, other philosophies. It is a theory of relativity among theories of absolute truth.

79 To most people it is a pleasure to conform and a pleasure to belong; existentialism is conspicuously unsuited to political or social subversion, since it is incapable of organized dogmatic resistance or formulations of resistance. It is capable only of one man's resistance; one personal expression of view; such as this book.

8

THE OBSESSION WITH MONEY

1 But the great majority of us do not live *by* any dogmatic philosophy—even when we claim that we do.
At most there are occasions when we act more or
less in accordance with some philosophy of which we
approve. Much more than we let philosophies guide
our lives, we allow obsessions to drive them; and
there is no doubt which has been the great driving
obsession of the last one hundred and fifty years.
It is money.

2 This obsession has a weakening effect on other philosophies, one that is very obvious if we look at the
comparative popularity of the various philosophies
since the French Revolution. The most successful
have been the most egalitarian; and the key philosophy of the nineteenth and twentieth centuries has
certainly been utilitarianism: the belief that the right
aim of human society is the greatest happiness of the
greatest number. All philosophies have now to sell
themselves, and in a very market-place sense. In
short, our obsession with money, the most obvious
and omnipresent source of inequality and therefore
unhappiness, colours all our beings and ways of
seeing life.

3 Having, not being, governs our time.

WEALTH AND POVERTY

4 The trial of money as the unique source of happiness
has begun, in the richer countries of the West; it will

fail. Wealth in itself is innocent. The rich man in himself is innocent. But wealth and rich men surrounded by poverty and poor men are guilty.

5 This tension, between the poles of poverty and wealth, is one of the most potent in our societies. It is so potent that many poor would rather remain poor with the chance of becoming rich than be neither poor nor rich with no chance of change.

6 Nothing differentiates more than wealth; nothing similarizes more than poverty. That is why we all want to be rich. We want to be different. Only money can buy both security and the variety we need. The dishonourable pursuit of money thus becomes also the honourable pursuit of both variety and security.

7 Money is potentiality; is control of, and access to, hazard; is freedom to choose; is power. The rich once thought they could buy their way into heaven; now heaven has moved to the here and now. But the rich man has not changed; and his belief that he can still buy his way into heaven-on-earth seems proved.

8 Both rich and poor countersupport the present disparity in the distribution of wealth. The more a political system equalizes the distribution of wealth, then the more popular become the ways of avoiding such equality.

9 Just as poor individuals countersupport rich individuals, so do poor countries countersupport the difference in wealth of the countries of the world. America and the West European countries are hated, but envied: and copied. A poor country is a rich one that is not rich.

10 Lotteries, football pools, bingo games and the rest
    are the chief protection of the modern rich against
    the furies of the modern poor. One hangs from the
    lamp-post the person one hates; not the person one
    wants to be.

11 We want money to buy those things that a good
    society would provide for nothing. That is, knowl-
    edge, understanding and experiencing; reading about
    the ends of the world and going to the ends of the
    world; not going through life not understanding most
    of what one sees, and therefore not seeing most of
    what one looks at. The terrible thing about poverty is
    less that it starves than that it stagnates as it starves.

12 Riches buy variety. That is the great law of capitalist
    societies. The only way to escape psychological frus-
    tration in them is to become rich. All the other exits
    are blocked.

13 It does not necessarily require any of the nobler
    human qualities to make money. So the making of
    money is a kind of equalizer. It becomes natural that
    a man should be judged by what he can get—money;
    and not by what he could never in any circumstances
    get if he was not born with it.

14 The dictionary calls money 'a medium of exchange'. I
    call it the human answer to the inhuman hazard that
    dominates existence. Genius, intellect, health, wis-
    dom, strength of will and body, good looks—all these
    are prizes we draw in the lottery that takes place be-
    fore our birth. Money is the makeshift human lottery
    that half compensates those who were unsuccessful in
    the first cosmic lottery. But money is a poor lottery,
    since the prizes won in the first prenatal lottery con-
    stitute a handsome free issue of tickets for the next.

If you are lucky in the first you are more likely to be lucky in the second.

15 The poor tolerate wealth in this order; most, wealth acquired after birth by pure luck; next, wealth fairly earned according to the current system; least of all, wealth acquired at birth, inherited wealth.

16 The supreme hazard is that I am who I am. The child of a Texan multi-millionaire, or of a Central African pygmy. Gamblers though we are, it sticks in our throats that this hazard is so pure and the apparent penalties and rewards are so enormously separate. But so effective in making the harsh reality tolerable is the analogy of the lottery that even the unfairest rewards and privileges will be countersupported. I believe the analogy is an evil one and all belief in it fundamentally ignoble. We behave like gamblers who make a virtue of accepting bad luck. We say, *Only one horse can win. It's all in the luck of the game. Someone must lose.* But these are descriptions, not prescriptions. We are not only gamblers, we are the horses they gamble on. Unlike real race-horses, we are not equally well treated, whether we win or lose. And we are not horses at all, since we can think, compare and communicate.

17 We are fellow members of the human race; not rivals in it. We are given intelligence and freedom to counteract and control the effects of the hazard that underlies all existence; not to justify injustice by them.

THE MONETIZATION OF PLEASURE

18 Once man believed he could make his own pleasures; now he believes he must pay for them. As if flowers

no longer grew in fields and gardens; but only in florists' shops.

19   Capitalist societies require a maximum opportunity for spending; both for inherent economic reasons and because the chief pleasure of the majority lies in spending. To facilitate this pleasure, hire-purchase systems are developed; the various forms of lottery fascinate the would-be rich as the brightly lit booths of a travelling fair once fascinated the country peasant. All those symptoms classed under consumer neurosis appear; but there is a far worse effect than all these.

20   This is the monetization of pleasure; the inability to conceive of pleasure except as being in some way connected with getting and spending. The invisible patina on an object is now its value, not its true intrinsic beauty. An experience is now something that has to be possessed as an object bought can be possessed; and even other human beings, husbands, wives, mistresses, lovers, children, friends, come to be possessed or unpossessed objects associated with values derived more from the world of money than from the world of humanity.

21   It is the possessor who is always the possessed. Our mania for collecting not only objects worth money but experiences that have cost money and our regarding of such a thesaurus of experiences as evidence of a valid existence (just as misers characteristically regard their hoarding as a virtue) finally make us poor in all but the economic sense. We seem to ourselves to live in exile from all we cannot afford. The pleasures that cost nothing come to seem worth nothing. Once we took our good deeds *to* heaven;

now we take our purchases and our expense accounts *as* heaven.

22 The shoddy-goods economy: workers must be paid to produce more and buy more. Much must be consumed and if much must be consumed, goods must be designed to last for as short a time as the guillible public will tolerate. The community craftsman disappears; he commits the archcrime of making lasting goods. Exit humans and creators, enter mechanics and machines. The mechanics want mechanical pleasures, of course; not human and creative ones.

23 The corollary vogue among the intelligentsia and bourgeoisie is for the antique; for the handmade, the solid, the distinctive, the durable; for the 'craft' shop, for goods made in countries too poor to afford machine production.

24 Entertainment at a low cost and everywhere cripples man's powers of self-pleasing. The mechanical receiver turns man into a mechanical receiver. We object to battery hens; but we are turning ourselves into battery humans.

25 In a town with too many men, prostitution becomes inevitable. Every pleasure experience becomes prostituted or prostitutable. The moneyed workers, those emancipated by social progress from proletariathood, lose all confidence in their own ability to amuse themselves and in their own taste. The price they pay for having money to spend is the surrender of their old working-class freedom in cultural matters to the skilled technological opinion-molders employed by commerce. Their labour is no longer exploited; but their minds are.

26 The aim of commerce has always been to market every pleasure possible and to sell it to as many as possible. The producer and the retailer are neutral, they claim no morality; they simply satisfy the public desire. But what we are being increasingly offered by commerce is not the pleasure, but a reproduction of it. Not the skylark singing in the hayfields, but a skylark in a record player; not a Renoir but a printed 'replica'; not the play in the theatre, but a 'television version' of it; not the real soup, but an 'instant' powder; not the Bermudas, but a documentary film of them.

27 It is the technical problems, not a lack of potential consumer demand, that stop us from having cans of tropical sunset, tubes of warm Pacific breezes, and packets of 'easy-mix' sexual pleasure. We are able to reproduce almost anything audible or visible; already someone has invented a jukebox for smells; and only Aldous Huxley's 'feelies' still seem completely out of our reach.*

28 The reasons for this demand that secondhand or imitation experience should be made as available as possible are obvious. Life has never seemed so short, but rich; and death so absolute. And if social and economic circumstances put many direct pleasures out of reach of the majority then they will naturally and reasonably take what substitute for the real thing they can get.

29 This monetization of pleasure is a makeshift means to get us through a period of history when the majority will not be able to have direct access to the things they want. As more and more realize what full being means and that their societies made it impossible for them to give this full being reality, the

marketing of reproduction and imitation sources of pleasure—substitutes for the real sources of pleasure —becomes more and more important.

30 We talk of consumer goods and consumer services; but these are in fact placebos society has increasingly to offer its members as they become aware that their real wants are largely caused by corrigible inadequacies of the social, political, international or human situation. In this field, all controllers of the dispensers of the placebos, that is, the governors, are in the same predicament, however far apart they may seem politically.

THE AUTOMATION VACUUM

31 Now a terrifying, because violently aggravating, new factor has appeared in this situation. It is cybernetics, the already advanced technique of controlling machines by other machines.

32 Man is about to be deprived of a great pole—work routine. The nightmare of the capitalist society is unemployment; the nightmare of the cybernetic society will be employment.

33 There have been absurd suggestions: that the disemployed masses must be forced to take part in compulsory games; that we shall have to undertake vast tasks, like the digging of canals and the moving of mountains, by primitive hand means; that the great majority must be sterilized. These proposals are ridiculous; but the potential quantity and intensity of frustration in a cybernetic society is terrifying.

34 There is surely only one acceptable solution. The

energy poured into the old work routine must be poured into new 'routines' of education, both learning and teaching, and enjoyment. Working for money, in order to be able to spend and enjoy, must become working for knowledge and the power to enjoy through knowledge.

35   Evolution is about to go over on to a new tack. A reorientation of purpose; a reacclimatization of man. The disappearance of the work routine will also mean the disappearance of the counterpole of much of the pleasure we feel. Most of us will, in capitalist or *laissez-faire* economic terms, be superseded and obsolete machines, requiring a fuel that no longer exists; like regular soldiers in a sudden and permanent peace.

36   The only persons who have been able to support endless free time without damaging society have until now been the polymath, the scholar, the scientist and the artist; the person of multiple culture. The only work that can never end is the pursuit and expression of knowledge.

37   The state of the future will not be the industrial state, and cannot be it, unless automation is retarded artificially. It must be the university state, and in the old sense of university: a state in which there are endless opportunities to acquire knowledge, where the educational system is the widest possible (of the type I propose in the ninth group of notes), where there are facilities, enjoyable to all, to learn and to create and to travel and to experience; where the element of hazard, of surprise, is incorporated into the social system; and where pleasure is not monetized.

38   Slave-owning societies of the past show the obvious

dangers facing a leisured class. They have been either stagnantly sybaritic or aggressively military. Leisure that has no other aim than the perpetuation of leisure breeds decadence or war, since peace and leisure need frequent purges. Soon, in much less than another hundred years, it will be the machines that are the slaves, and slaves that cannot revolt; and all humanity will then be potentially the leisured class. But we are long past the age of clysters and bleeding.

39 Evolution seems always to seize on some such force as the obsession with money, because it is easier to organize life when there is such a force on hand. Such forces invariably land mankind in the Midas Situation —almost literally so, in this case. The lust to find cheaper methods of production, such as automation, finally destroys the lust itself. We chase the reward, we get the reward; and then we discover that the true reward is always the next reward. Automation may seem an end in itself, just as buying pleasure may; but these false ends in themselves simply take us to where we can see they are not.

THE DUTIES OF LEISURE

40 That leisure seems to have no duties is precisely what puritans object to in it; the puritan fallacy is that there is something intrinsically noble in work. This historically explicable need to enhance the value of work really undertaken only in order to get wages has created a climate in which too much external pleasure and enjoyment very quickly cloy. It is a mistake to think that a man who has been long conditioned to enjoy three weeks' holiday a year is necessarily happier when he is suddenly given six. Whatever situation we are in we try to derive some relativity of recom-

pense from it; and so in a condition without, for a stranger, any possibility of happiness a habitué will find some happiness. Indeed, he is almost certainly a habitué because he has found rewards in the condition. Our ability to enjoy is conditioned by the situation in which we have had to learn to enjoy.

41 The first duty of having leisure is thus to learn to enjoy it; and this seems to me enormously more difficult than the optimists would have us believe. No union has yet called its members out on strike for less wages and longer hours; but the day may come.

42 The second duty of having leisure is more like one of the old duties. It is to share one's leisure, that is, to give some of it to those who still have insufficient leisure.

43 Poverty is the counterpole that drives us now; soon it will be ignorance. The hungry brain, not the hungry belly; lack of knowledge and experience, not lack of food. A society of leisure must to begin with be a minority society. The counterpole of ignorance will be easily found outside its frontiers. The chief function of the first leisure societies will be the education, improvement and enleisurement of the backward societies of the world. There cannot be any true leisure until all the world possesses it equally.

44 This is the great change that must take place in human history. The rich societies must give away not only their surplus money, but their surplus leisure and their surplus capacity to educate.

45 These things will never come to be without planning; above all planning and reorientating our systems of education. Shaw (in *Major Barbara*) saw the point-

lessness of expecting any moral progress before economic advancement has been achieved. In some countries that economic advancement has now largely been achieved; yet there is no sign of any change in the educational systems. They are still geared to the necessities of the first stage—to Andrew Undershaft's insistence on concrete economic achievement; not to his daughter Barbara's vision of a proper human education.

DEATH BY NUMBERS

46 Over all this obsession with money, this lust for an equal happiness, hangs the black cloud of the world population rate. This is the ultimate horror in our present situation.

47 At current birthrates the population of the world will have doubled in fifty years. Therefore in the lifetimes of many of us every problem caused by overpopulation—big-city neurosis, traffic problems, famine, inflation, foul air, the annihilation of nature, the regimentation of the individual—all these will be at least doubly intense. In this context the human and economic wealth poured into space travel and the nuclear arms race is the most stupendous example of fiddling while civilization burns in the history of man.

48 There are two kinds of objection to the controlled reduction of population; one, that such control is morally bad, and the other, that it is evolutionarily wrong.

49 The opposers on moral grounds are of three principal kinds: religious, political and individualist.

50 There were formerly very dubious ecclesiastical reasons for encouraging a high birthrate: more of the faithful were born, and large families created or perpetuated the kind of economic situation in which poverty, ignorance and despair drove the victims into the 'sanctuary' of the church. But such policies worked only in priest-dominated environments, and these have largely ceased to exist except in a few backward countries.

51 A much more convincing religious argument is this: birth-control practices encourage private promiscuity and in particular adultery. It is difficult to deny this, but equally difficult to show that the suppression of birth-control practices (the repression of private promiscuity) would bring a stabler society. The flood current of evolution is set for sexual freedom. It is no longer a question of damming it up; but of controlling the flood. And this is a flood of something much more dangerous than water.

52 Some religious people still believe that birth-control practices are contrary to divine will. But the 'divine will' is not against life insurance boards, or parapets, or insecticides, or surgery, or computers, or antiseptics, or sea walls, or fire brigades. Why does it allow these forms of scientific control (some abusable) of the hazards of life, and not birth control?

53 Another absurd religious argument is this: prophylaxis is murder, since it prevents the unconceived child from being conceived. But this doctrine, even if one accepts its premise (that we exist before we are conceived), raises considerable problems. There are a thousand ways of preventing a child being conceived without resorting to specific prophylaxis. Should husbands go away on business? Are they mur-

dering every conception-phase night they are away from home? Are all copulatory positions except the most apt for conception murder?

54 We can stop babies being conceived; but we cannot murder unconceived babies. All law requires a body.

55 We are given freedom so that we may control; and there cannot be special fields in which control is totally forbidden; in which, in short, we are condemned not to be free.

56 The opposers on political grounds say this: a powerful state needs a large population, and the higher the birthrate the more soldiers and workers it will have.

57 Since the advent of atomic weapons it is clear that what matters militarily is not number but know-how; this situation was already apparent as soon as the first machine gun was invented. Even from the point of view of conventional military requirements every country in the world today, including those with the most overseas commitments, is overpopulated.

58 Since automation, it is quite apparent that the unskilled workers of the world must become increasingly redundant. A conservative 1967 estimate of the current redundancy in highly industrialized countries was *one in every four workers.*

59 It is only in unmechanized peasant economies such as those in India that large families can be argued to be a necessity; and even if the argument is granted, clearly they are a necessity only for as long as the world allows such economies to be unmechanized.

60 The opposers on individualist grounds say this: choice

of size of family is one of the last free choices left to
adults in civilized society. To oblige them to limit the
size of their families would be the surrender of the
final citadel of the individual. I find such arguments
the most attractive; and yet they collapse before the
pressure of reality. For this kind of decision, to have
or not have a certain number of children, is far more
than a merely personal one. If this man and his wife
decide to have a family of six, then they are making
decisions that affect their society and their world far
beyond the furthest scope of their own rights as individuals, and indeed far beyond their own existences.

61 As American sociologists have discovered, an ominous by-product of economic prosperity is that it
turns the extra child into a desirable and affordable
adjunct of the affluent life. From there it becomes a
symbol of affluence, of success in life. The large family
has always been encouraged by politicians and
priests; the idolatry of those great gods Virility and
Fecundity is easily induced. But surely the extra child
is, in a world of starving children, the one luxury the
already fortunate affluent have no right to offer themselves. For if we claim we are free to breed like
rabbits, then evolution will see that we die like them.

62 There remains the second category of opposers: those
who claim that it is evolutionally wrong to control
population. There is a generational selfishness: let our
children look out for themselves. There is a better
argument. It is this: our capacity to multiply ourselves goes, and is meant to go, hand in hand with
our capacity to feed ourselves. But according to this
breed-and-brave-it theory if we are all to remain
healthy we must remain in a state of acute crisis. We
should build all our boats with a hole in the bottom—
then pump.

63 Even if we could feed a population twice the size of the present world population, and feed them better than they are fed now, there is no likelihood that such an overpopulated world would be happier than a properly populated one. *People need more than food, and all the other things they need flourish best when the crowd is least; that is, peace, education, space, and individuality.*

64 The future will surely see our apathy over population control as the greatest folly of our time. They will see that a vast structure in our societies was totally unnecessary, a mere product of having too many mouths to feed, too many hands to keep occupied. But above all they will see that the state of over-population turns progress into regress. How many modern inventions, how many economic theories, are really not progressive, but simply desperate attempts to stop up the leaks in the sinking boat? How much ingenuity and energy is poured into keeping us afloat instead of moving forwards?

CONCLUSION

65 Money-obsessed societies produce dissatisfied men and women because power to buy is as habit-forming, and finally as pernicious, as heroin. One is dead before one has enough. They produce guilty men, because too few have too much, and too many are savagely punished for their innocent poverty and ignorance. Behind each shilling, each franc, each mark, rouble, dollar is the stick-limbed child, the future, the envious and famished world to come.

66 Scientifically we know more of one another, and yet, like the receding galaxies, we seem to become each

lonelier, remoter. So most of us concentrate, in an
apparently meaningless and only too evidently precarious universe, on extracting as much pleasure for
ourselves as we can. We act as if we were born into
the death cell; condemned to a dangerous age, to an
inevitable holocaust; to a being whose only significant
aspects are that it is ludicrously brief and ends in a
total extinction of the power to enjoy. What hollows
us operates, like an awl, in two directions simulta-
neously. We have not only an exasperating inability to
get all that we want but also the excoriating counter-
cutting fear that what we want to get is, in terms of a
dimly glimpsed but far richer human reality, worthless. Never were there so many hollow people in the
world, like a huge and mounting shore of empty
cockleshells.

67 Everywhere we see the need for change; and in so
few places the satisfaction of that need. I come now
to the vital factor. It is education.

9

A NEW EDUCATION

1 At present almost all our education is directed to two
ends: to get wealth for the state and to gain a livelihood for the individual. It is therefore little wonder
that society is money-obsessed, since the whole tenor
of education seems to indicate that this obsession is
both normal and desirable.

2 In spite of the fact that we now have almost universal
education, we are qualitatively one of the least-
educated ages, precisely because education has everywhere surrendered to economic need. Relatively far
better educations were received by the fortunate few
in the eighteenth century; in the Renaissance; in
ancient Rome and Greece. The aims of education in
all those periods were far superior to our own; they
opened the student admirably to the understanding
and enjoyment of life and to his responsibilities towards society. Of course the facts and subjects of the
old classical education are largely unnecessary to us
today; and of course it was the product of a highly
unjust economic situation, but at its best it arrived at
something none of our present systems remotely approach: the rounded human being.

3 There should be four main aims in a good education.
The first is the one that pre-empts all present systems:
the training of the pupil for an economic role in
society. The second is teaching the nature of society
and the human polity. The third is teaching the
richness of existence. And the fourth is the establish-

141

ment of that sense of relative recompense which man, in contrast to the other orders of animate life, has so long lost. In simpler terms, we need to fit the students for a livelihood, then for living among other human beings, then for enjoying his own life, and finally for comprehending the purpose (and ultimately, the justice) of existence in human form.

4 Now there are two important distinctions between the first and the latter three of these aims. From the point of view of the state they are to a certain extent hostile. The economy does not want too much attention paid by its workers to social purpose, self-enjoyment and the ultimate nature of existence; it needs intelligent and obedient cogs, not intelligent and independent individuals. And since the state always has a very large say in the nature of the educational system, we can expect little desire for change from politicians and administrators.

5 The second distinction is this: whereas the first economic-role type of education will plainly vary with the economic needs of the nation, and so legitimately vary from country to country, the latter three purposes hardly vary at all, since we are all in the same human situation and endowed with the same senses. In these three fields virtually the same education could be taught all over the world; and should be taught. But this again represents a threat to the identity of the state; and is a second reason why its 'servants' can be expected to oppose any introduction of a universally similar syllabus.

6 Now it may be argued that the best of our universities, at least in the richer and culturally more advanced countries, already provide such an education. Oxford and Cambridge, Harvard and Yale, the great

new Californian universities, the Sorbonne and the Ecole Normale, and similar prestigious centres of learning certainly provide a richness of culture where a student *can* achieve those further three aims if he has the inclination and can find the time. But even here the overriding factor is the examination system. It is only in very recent times that the chief function of a university (or school of any kind) has been taken to be the grading of its students by examination. We know why this is so: to ensure that the most deserving students get the places available. But this immediately reveals the examination system for what it is: a desperate expedient, exactly analogous to rationing food in wartime, in a desperate situation.

7 All the evils of history are attributable to a shortage of schools. And the shortage of schools in our own time is the most desperate in the history of man. The more equality we want, the more education we want; the more means of communication, the more we see the want; the more leisure we gain, the more we need to be taught to use it; and the more populations grow, the more schools they will demand.

8 Each age has a special risk. Ours is letting half the world starve literally and nine-tenths of it starve educationally. No species can afford to be ignorant. The only world in which it could allow itself such a luxury is one in which it had no enemies and had risen above hazard and evolution.

A UNIVERSAL LANGUAGE

9 Before we can approach the concept of a universal education, we have to consider that of a universal language. Teaching is above all communication, and communication is impossible unless there is a gener-

ally understood medium. We therefore need a language that may be taught as a universal second tongue.

10 It is absolutely clear that the attempts to create such a language artificially (Esperanto, Ido and the rest) have failed. Their inventors' perhaps worthy desire to satisfy national pride by running together disparate elements from different languages leads them all into an absurd impracticability, since one thus destroys any hope of providing teachers who speak the language naturally; there is no existing and tried model to refer to for new developments and resources; and perhaps worst of all, these pseudo-languages can offer no literature.

11 There are four requisites of a universal language:
    1. It should be based on an already existing major language.
    2. It should be analytic, not synthetic. (Synthetic languages are those that incorporate signs as to meaning and syntactical function inside each word—that is, they have genders, case systems, a widely variable word order; analytic languages have fewer such features and depend far more on a rigorous word order.)
    3. It should have a phonetic spelling system based on a limited number of symbols.
    4. It should be able to provide an effective simple or basic mode of communication and a fertile and adaptable more complex one.

12 We may at once rule out the numerically most spoken language: Chinese. Its reading symbols are hopelessly unlimited; its pronunciation is tonal (meaning may depend on musical pitch); it is highly dialectal; and it is semantically, as every translator of Chinese poetry knows, bewilderingly imprecise.

13 With one exception all the principal European languages, whether Romance, Teutonic or Slavonic in origin, retain too many synthetic features in syntax and declension. The same is true of Arabic. However interesting and evocative gender-systems and complex verb and noun forms may be in a literary sense, philologically they are redundant. No one designing a new language with ease of learning and functional utility in mind would for a moment retain them.

14 This leads to the inescapable conclusion that the most suitable candidate is English. It is already the *de facto* second language of the world; and every teacher of languages knows that this is because it is the least synthetic of the major tongues and therefore the easiest to learn. If we British and Americans suppose that it has gained its ubiquity simply because of our past and present political power we are much mistaken. Foreigners increasingly speak English because it is the best tool available; not because they love or admire us.

15 Its advantages are considerable. It is numerically the second most spoken (as a mother-tongue) language of the world, and the most widely spoken by non-native speakers. Its dialects, unlike those of Chinese, are largely intercomprehensible. It has a rich literature, both historical and contemporary; and it has rich resources and a facility for new development. Its alphabet is simple. And it is very well suited to both simple and complex modes of expression.

16 It has, of course, disadvantages. Its spelling is (compared to a language like Italian) very far from phonetic. It does retain some synthetic features, including some annoying irregularities in declension. In some of its spoken forms (such as British English) it be-

comes almost a tonal language, full of subtle nuances of meaning dependent on minute (for a foreigner) changes of stress. Its richness of vocabulary—two or three times more words than most other European languages—also creates problems of usage.

17   But the adaptations required are not too forbidding —or if they are so, only to those of us for whom English is the mother-tongue. The most urgent need is for a phonetic spelling system (which would of course do something far more important than facilitate spelling: is would aid pronunciation). No one has ever fully answered Bernard Shaw's arguments for this step. The rationalization of the present alphabet is a small price to pay for the vastly increased utility it would give to the language.

18   The second field for improvement lies in the regularization of exceptions in declension and syntax. This is a far more difficult problem, especially as so many of the exceptions lie among very common words. One has only to regularize a sentence like 'I saw the men working hard' into 'I seed the mans working hardly' to realize the pitfalls. Nonetheless there are many declensional sore thumbs that could be remedied without fear of ambiguity.

19   Language is a tool, the most important that man has. We should allow nothing—neither the prejudice of the linguistic chauvinists nor our (if we are English) distaste for barbaric-sounding innovations in our language—to stand in the way of a unilingual world. This is in a sense an English-speakers' responsibility. We should perfect the tool for the special function. All the evidence is that the rest of the world will happily learn to use it.

THE THREE FURTHER AIMS
OF EDUCATION

20   Education is the most vital of all social activities and
therefore the most eagerly abused by the contemporary power-system—whether that system is religious, as in the Middle Ages, or political-economic, as
for the last century or so. It has in fact been tyrannized since the rise of the great religions in the first
millennium. In many ways the educational theories
of the ancients are more modern—less corrupted by
political and economic need—than any that have
been evolved since, and the three further aims of
education I propose are not mine. They were laid
down in the third century after Christ by the great
Neo-Platonist philosopher, Plotinus. He required an
outward education—civil and social; an inward one
—personal and self-revealing; and finally a synoptic
education that would allow the student to grasp, or
at least glimpse, the complex whole of human existence. This is not the place to develop in any detail
the scheme of such a triple education in humanity;
but some general needs and problems must be dealt
with. The first and most practical difficulty in establishing a world-wide syllabus in humanity is only too
clearly nationalism.

NATIONALISM

21   Nationalism is a cheap instinct and a dangerous tool.
Take away from any country what it owes to other
countries; and then be proud of it if you can.

22   In a poor country, patriotism is to believe that one's
country would be the best if it were rich and power-

ful. In a rich one, patriotism is to believe that one's country is the best because it is rich and powerful. So patriotism becomes the desire to get what others have or to keep others from getting what one has. In short, it is an aspect of conservatism; of animal envy and animal selfishness.

23 The significant truth is not that you are lucky to have been born into one of the best—the richest or most powerful—countries; but that others are unlucky not to have been born into it. You are not a starving Indian peasant, but you might have been. That you are not is not a matter for self-congratulation, but one for charitable action, for concern. The proper domain for nationalism is art and culture; not politics.

24 Men were one in a tribe, one in a city, were one in a church, in a political party. But now they are becoming a world of isolated ones. The old bonds dissolve; the bonds of the race, of the shared language, of the shared rites, of the shared history. This is good. We disintegrate now to integrate in the only good unity: a one humanity.

25 An education in humanity must inculcate a oneness of situation in each mind in each land: a common predicament and a common existence, a common right to recompense, and a common justification and justice. It must therefore teach children to see the faults in society; by teaching them for nationalistic reasons to pretend that bad things are good, we teach them to teach the same. A bad lesson has a long life.

26 *What the state or the system considers a good teacher and what is a good teacher are always two different things. A good teacher never teaches only his subject.*

27 It has never been more important that we should have such teachers; and this is because we now know that in another fifty years' time the great bulk of our teaching will be done by machines. To those who can conceive of education only as the learning of facts and techniques that will be useful to the economic system, this prospect is excellent. No human teacher will be able to equal a well-programmed computer-teacher in his command of the science of his subject, or in his efficiency as an imparter of information.

28 I referred to this mechanistic heresy in the discussion of Christianity. *But the best method is the most effective one for the situation, not the most efficient in theory.* The menace facing us in the near future is that we shall be ourselves mechanized into believing that the good teacher is the most efficient in terms of the facts of his subject. If we believe this, then we shall fall under the tyranny of our computers—in short, under the worst, because universal, form of nationalism in the history of man.

29 But not all is black in this prospect. There are many fields in which we can welcome the computer-teacher; and that will free the human teachers for the teaching of the subjects (perhaps it would be better to say *method of teaching*) where they cannot be supplanted. And one of the prime purposes of the triple education in humanity I am advocating will be to counteract, or place in perspective, the triumph of the computer in its appropriate fields.

ART AND SCIENCE

30 This specific problem of the computer-teacher leads to the next great problem: that of the proper roles of science and art in human life.

31 Everyone should have a sound grounding in all the fundamental sciences, and all should know the great linchpin, the axis of reason, that is, scientific method. But large areas of science are remote from the ordinary business of living, and I would define the areas most relevant to education in humanity as those that destroy prejudice, superstition and the kind of ignorance that is clearly harmful to society. In March, 1963, hundreds of Balinese were killed in a volcanic eruption because they would not leave their homes. They believed that the gods would punish anyone who ran away. Our world spends millions on exploring planets we already know to be uninhabitable and yet lets such lethal stupidity still brew on Earth.

32 Science has two principal effects on its practitioners. One, totally beneficial, is heuristic—that is, it trains the scientist to think and discover for himself. Plainly we need as much education in this aspect of science as we can get. But another characteristic of science is double-edged, and this is its tendency to analyse, to break down the whole into components. Now plainly analysis is a very vital part of the heuristic process; but its side-effects, as in some medicines, may be extremely pernicious.

33 The purely analytic scientist becomes so accustomed to seeing matter as a demonstration of certain verifiable or falsifiable principles that he lives at one remove from it. Between him and the real world springs the law, the explanation, the necessity to categorize. Everything Midas touched turned to gold, everything this kind of scientist touches turns to its function in his analysis.

34 There is another allied danger. The complexity of the modern sciences is such that specialization is essen-

tial; not only in the interests of scientific or industrial efficiency, but in the nature of the mind's capacity. The scholar in many fields is extinct; not because the desire to be such a scholar is extinct, but because the *fields* are too many, and too complex.

35 Pure science and impure economics both require of the scientist that he should live most of his thinking life along some spoke remote from the true hub of society of which he is a member; and from the true hub of the now in which he is. This produces the characteristic and expectable two-facedness of the modern scientist: scientific morality and social immorality. Scientists have an inherent tendency to become slaves of the state.

36 The scientific mind, in being totally scientific, is being unscientific. We are in a phase of history where the scientific pole is dominant; but where there is pole, there is counterpole. The scientist atomizes, someone must synthesize; the scientist withdraws, someone must draw together. The scientist particularizes, someone must universalize. The scientist dehumanizes, someone must humanize. The scientist turns his back on the as yet, and perhaps eternally, unverifiable; and someone must face it.

37 Art, even the simplest, is the expression of truths too complex for science to express, or to conveniently express. This is not to say that science is in some way inferior to art, but that they have different purposes and different uses. Art is a human shorthand of knowledge, a crucible, an algebra, a tremendous condensing in the case of great art of galaxies of thoughts, facts, memories, emotions, events, experiences, to ten lines in *Macbeth,* to six bars in Bach, to a square foot of canvas in a Rembrandt.

38   Certain scientific laws may seem analogous to great
     art; they condense countless trillions of phenomena
     into one statement. But this statement is an abstrac-
     tion, not a concentration, of reality.

39   All arts tend to become sciences, or crafts; but the
     essential mystery in art is that the artist constantly
     surpasses whatever the science or the craft of the art
     might have foretold; and constantly surpasses the
     scientific description and evaluation of what is art
     and what is good or bad art.

40   Art is always a complex beyond science. It computes
     all the computers. One might feed the tastes of a thou-
     sand musical people into a computer, which could
     then compose 'their' music; but it would deny the
     great principle—an artefact is pre-eminently what-
     ever only one man could have made. It is a statement
     of *one in the face of* all; not a statement *by one for
     the use of* all.*

41   Science is what a machine can or might do; art is
     what it will never do. This is a definition of what art
     should and *must* be to mankind; not a denial of the
     already proven fact that science can perfectly well
     manufacture what can pass as art.

42   A good scientist cuts the umbilical cord between his
     private personality, his emotions, his self, and his
     creation; his discovery of a new law, or phenomenon,
     or property. But a good artefact is always a limb,
     a branch, a second self. Science disembodies; art em-
     bodies.

43   It is tempting to treat artefacts as phenomena that
     can be best apprehended when scientifically analysed
     and classified; thence the sciences of art history and

of criticism. From this springs the illusion that all art is contained within the science that can describe, appraise and categorize it; thence, the ridiculous belief that art is finally 'inferior' to science, as if nature is inferior to natural history.

44 This scientization of art, so characteristic of our age, is absurd. Science has shaken off the fetters of art, and now fetters art. Above all it scientizes the inmost characteristic of art—mystery. For what good science tries to eliminate, good art seeks to provoke— mystery, which is lethal to the one, and vital to the other.

45 Of course I do not wish to deny the utility of a scientific criticism, a natural history, of art. But I should like to see destroyed the notion that art is a pseudo-science; that it is sufficient to *know* art; that art is knowable in the sense that an electronic circuit or a rabbit's foetus is knowable.

46 Different tools and languages; different superficial notions of what is vital in existence, therefore different superficial aims; different minds; yet all great scientists are in a sense artists and all great artists are in a sense scientists, since they have the same human aim: to approach a reality, to convey a reality, to symbolize a reality, to summarize a reality, to convince of a reality. All serious scientists and artists want the same: a truth that no one will need to change.

47 All symbolization, and all science and all art is symbolization, is an attempt to escape from time. All symbols summarize; evoke what is absent; serve as tools; permit us to control our movements in the river of time, and are thus attempts to control time.

But science tries to be true of an event for all time; while art tries to be an event for all time.

48 Neither the scientifically nor the artistically expressed reality is the most real reality. The 'real' reality is a meaningless particularity, a total incoherence, a ubiquitous isolation, a universal disconnection. It is a sheet of blank paper; we do not call the drawings or equations we make on the paper the paper. Our interpretations of reality are not 'the' reality, any more than the blankness of the paper is the drawing. Our drawings, our equations, are ultimately pseudo-realities, but those are the only realities that concern us because they are the only realities that can concern us.

49 The practice of an art, or arts, is as essential to the whole man as a knowledge of science. This is not because of what art is but because of what art does to the artist.

50 All artefacts please and teach the artist first, and other people later. The pleasing and teaching come from the explanation of self by the expression of self; by seeing the self, and all the selves of the whole self, in the mirror of what the self has created.

51 In any good education science and art must hold equal rank. They do not hold equal rank today because the majority of scientists are not true scientists, that is heuristic pursuers of knowledge, but technologists, or analytical appliers of it. The technological view of life is one that of its nature imposes a highly mechanical and empirical approach within its own field; the danger now is that this approach is made to all other fields as well. And to the human turned technologist art must seem a highly dismissible ac-

tivity because neither it nor its effects can be assessed by any easily verifiable method.

52 The true scientist never dismisses, depreciates, or condescends to art; I consider this an almost fundamental definition of him. And conversely, of the true artist.

53 Already, in America especially, we see the attempt to turn art into a kind of pseudo-technology. In the hideously misnamed 'creative writing' courses the notion is spread that it is sufficient to learn the technique to achieve the value, and there are now increasing hosts of writers and painters characterized by a very distinctive pseudo-technological hollowness.

54 Their artefacts are cleverly assembled and fashionably neat, neatly fashionable, and yet the whole is never more than the sum of the parts. When the technique is praised, everything is praised. There is a spotless eggshell, but no meat.

55 Of course most good and all great artists show skill at techniques. But the pseudo-technological artist is like an angler who thinks the essential is to be able to handle a rod and bait a hook; but the true essential is to know a river to fish in. The thing comes first, then its expression; and today we are faced with an army of cleverly-trained expressers all in pursuit of something to express; a crowd of expert anglers futilely casting in the middle of a ploughed field.

56 A counter argument is this: granted that the ability to express is not the same as the expression of something valuable, a person trained to express is still better equipped to perceive the valuably expressible than an untrained one. I believe the contrary: that the teaching of command of special techniques limits vision

rather than extends it. If you train someone to be an angler using special techniques, he will see the world in terms of angling by those special techniques.

57 A young would-be artist trained to 'create' in the style of this or that successful modern artist will begin to gain that artist's sensibility as well as his techniques; and this always present but never so probable prospect of being endlessly imitated, of endlessly imposing his sensibilities and views of life on impressible young 'trained' minds, must seem one of the most disagreeable facing the genuinely serious and gifted artist.

58 Being an artist is first discovering the self and then stating the self in self-chosen terms. The proper school of any art should have two courses: a museum course and a craft course. The museum course simply teaches the history of the art and the monuments (all past masters) of the art; the craft course teaches the basic practical essentials, the syntax, grammar, prosody, paint mixing, academic draughtsmanship, harmony, instrumental ranges, and the rest. All teaching or advocating of a style, a sensibility, a philosophy, is pernicious; is pseudo-technology, not art.

59 Show the young sailor how to sail; but don't so falsify the compass and the chart that he can sail only in one direction.

60 To be an artist is not to be a member of a secret society; it is not an activity inscrutably forbidden to the majority of mankind. Even the clumsiest, ugliest and most ignorant lovers make love; and what is important is the oneness of man in making artefacts, not the abyss said to exist between a Leonardo and the average of mankind. We are not all to be Leonardos; but of the same kind as Leonardo, for genius is only

one end of the scale. I climbed Parnassus once, and between the mundane village of Arachova at the foot and the lovely summit, quite as lovely as the poets have always had it to be, there is nothing but a slope; no abyss, no cliff, no place where wings are necessary.

61   A child is not excused from games and physical training because he is not brilliant at them. Only one child in ten cannot be taught music. Poetry has nothing to do with recitation, with learning by heart or reading texts for examination purposes. Poetry is saying what you are in words in rhythmic patterns. Visual art is the same, but in shapes and colours instead of words.

62   An artist, as we understand the word today, is someone who does by nature what we should all do by education. But all our modern technology-biased systems of education concentrate far too much on the science of art, that is, art history and art categorization and art appreciation, and far too little on the personal creation of artefacts; as if diagrams, discussions, photographs and films of games and physical exercise were an adequate substitute for the real thing. *It is useless to provide endless facilities for the enjoyment of other people's art unless there are corresponding facilities for creating one's own.*

63   Freedom is inherent in the best art, as it is in the best science. Both are essentially demolishers of tyranny and dogma; are melters of petrifaction, breakers of the iron situation. To begin with, an artist may oppose merely because he has the power to express opposition; and then one day his own expressed opposition expresses him. His art enlists him. The poem I write today writes me tomorrow. I find the scientific law; and then the law finds me.

GAMES

64 Games, sports and pastimes that require rules and social contact have become increasingly significant in the last century. It was calculated that something like one hundred and fifty *million* people watched on television the final of the football World Cup in 1966. As with art, we may tend to regard games as a rather unimportant leisure activity. But as leisure increases, so does their influence on our lives.

65 Games are far more important to us, and in far deeper ways, than we like to admit. Some psychologists explain all the symbolic values we attach to games, and to losing and winning them, in Freudian terms. Football consists of twenty-two penises in pursuit of a vagina; a golf club is a steel-shafted phallus; the chess king and queen are Laius and Jocasta; all winning is a form either of evacuation or of ejaculation; and so on. Such explanations may or may not have value in discussing the origin of the game. But for most players and spectators a much more plausible explanation is the Adlerian one, that a game is a system for achieving superiority. It is moreover a system (like money getting) that is to a certain extent a human answer to the inhuman hazard of the cosmic lottery; to be able to win at a game compensates the winner for not being able to win outside the context of the game. This *raison d'être* of the game is most clearly seen in the games of pure chance; but many other games have deliberate hazards; and even in games technically free of hazards the bounce, the lie, the fly in the eye exist. The evil is this: from instituting this system of equalizing hazard man soon moves to regarding the winner in

it as not merely lucky but in some way excellent; just as he now comes to regard the rich man as in some way intrinsically excellent.*

66 The prestige coveters have always tried to seize sport as their province. This is especially so in times of peace. Much has been made of the nobility of the early Olympic Games, in the sixth and seventh centuries before Christ, and of their later corruption under the Romans. But the sprig of olive was already too large a prize. Competition, the need to keep equal and the drive to do better, haunts mankind. But there are plenty of real fields for competition without inventing artificial ones.

67 Sport is an opportunity for personal pleasure, a situation where beauty may arise. But what is being contested is never prestige. Simply the game. The winner has more skill or more luck; by winning he is not in any sense in any game necessarily a better human being than the loser.

68 Almost all the great popular sports of the world come from Britain. But what Britain has not been able to export is the amateur ethos of the game. Most foreigners, and now many Britons, want to win at any cost within the rules; and they keep to the rules only because a game without rules is war.

69 There are means-orientated societies, for whom the game is the game; and ends-orientated societies, for whom the game is winning. In the first, if one is happy, then one is successful; in the second, one cannot be happy unless one is successful. The whole tendency of evolution and history suggests that man must become means-orientated if he is to survive.

70 The primary function of all the great human activities
—art, science, philosophy, religion—is to bring man
nearer the truth. Not to win, not to beat another
team, not to be invincible. The contemporary fuss
about amateurs and professionals is nothing. Any
sportsman who plays mainly in order to win, that is,
mainly not for the pleasure of playing, is a professional. He may not want money, but he wants prestige, and prestige of this sort is as dirty as gold.

CULPABILITY

71 It is an old saying that crime depends on society; and
no doubt the cynical answer, that society depends on
crime, is equally old. One of the grimmest modern
statistical facts is that not only is crime on the increase, but even on the increase relative to the population increase. And the problem of culpability is,
to both society and to an education in humanity, of
very far from academic significance.

72 There are two extreme views. One is that all criminals
have complete free will; the other is that they have
none. We live socially in accordance with the first
belief; most of us, as individuals, tend to believe in
the second.

73 A judge says to a criminal: *the crime you have committed is a dastardly one.* But he should say: *the
action you have done has harmed society, and is a
sign that you have a diseased or deficient mind; I
apologize to you in the name of society, if insufficient
education is to blame, and I sympathize with you as a
fellow human, if hereditary factors are to blame; I
will now ensure that you have the best possible treatment and care.* In the world as it is, no judge would
dare to be so preposterously humane because he

knows perfectly well that a judge is a dispenser of law, not of justice. We speak of the policy of the nuclear deterrent as if it is a terrible one to have to live under. But ever since the institution of law we have lived under a policy of the deterrent; not under a true human justice. An offer to try to cure is certainly not a sufficient practical deterrent to crime; but neither is a total refusal to try to cure a sufficient social response. There is a mean; and at present we are nowhere near it.

74   A sick man can reasonably hate society for sending him to prison; but not to hospital.

75   In a truly just world, cupability would clearly be a scientific, not a moral, calculation. No society is innocent of the crimes committed in it; we know very well that we call the biologically innocent legally guilty simply for convenience. The old argument here is this: if people start believing they cannot help committing crimes they will start committing those they could have desisted from.

76   But if we concede that a great majority of criminals are not responsible for their crimes, which are really committed by factors over which they have no control (genes, environment, lack of education), the way is free to treat them as we treat any other person who is seriously ill. In genetics we are still helpless; but we can control environment and education. And the education in humanity, which must be designed to alleviate a chief cause of all crime, the sense of inequality that makes social irresponsibility almost a courageous revolutionary gesture, is plainly best suited to establishing such control.

77   An important obstacle to the prevention and proper

treatment of criminals is the emotional way in which
we view 'sin' and 'crime'. The one is of course a
legacy of Christianity; and the other of Greek-Roman
law. Both concepts are thoroughly outmoded and
widely harmful.

78 They disseminate a shared myth: that an evil deed
can be paid for. In one case by penance and remorse;
in the other, by accepting punishment. Remorse gives
a pleasurable and masochistic illusion that one is,
though superficially evil, fundamentally good. Penance and punishment (which share the same root ety-
mologically) appear, when they are completed, simply to define the correct ownership of the crime—
and very often its proceeds. *I have paid for my house*
and *I have paid for my crime* are unhappily similar
sentences in their implication.

79 Sin throws an aura of impermissibility round many
pleasures. In other words, it glamourizes and
heightens them, since to forbid or deny any pleasure
greatly increases its enjoyability, on both physical and
psychological grounds. The chief ranters against 'sin'
in history can be numbered among its leading coun-
tersupporters. 'Crime', in the free-will significance
law attaches to the word, is merely a legal equivalent
of the religious term.

80 It is of use to examine the existentialist position on
culpability. An existentialist says: As well as my good
actions, I am my past bad actions; I cannot deny
them; if I ignore their having taken place, I am a
coward, a child; I can only accept them. From this
some modern writers have argued that by deliberately
committing a crime and deliberately, without remorse,
accepting that I have committed a crime, I can best
demonstrate my own existing as a unique individual

and my rejection of the world of the others, that is, hypocritical organized society. But this is a romantic perversion of existentialism. I prove I exist not by making senseless decisions or committing deliberate crimes in order that they may be 'accepted' and then constitute a proof of the 'authenticity' and uniqueness of my existence, because by so acting I establish nothing but my own particular sense of inadequacy in face of external social reality; but I prove I exist by using my acceptance of past and bad actions as a source of energy for the improvement of my future actions or attitudes inside that reality.

81 Existentialism says, in short, that if I commit an evil then I must live with it for the rest of my life; and that the only way I can live with it is by accepting that it is always present in me. Nothing, no remorse, no punishment, can efface it; and therefore each new evil I do is not a relapse, a replacement, but an addition. Nothing cleans the slate; it can become only dirtier.

82 This view of crime is invaluable because it encourages freedom of will; it allows the criminal to believe he can choose, he can shape and balance his life, he can try to be his own master. Joined with the help to be given by psychiatry, it offers the criminal his best chance of never coming back through the prison gates when he is released. We need to ban the dreadful ogres of penal law and penitential religion from our prisons; and we need to regard the period immediately after release in the same way as we regard the same period after a stay in hospital. It is one of convalescence; and no released prisoner should be expected to be capable of immediate normal function in society. He will need economic and psychological support.

83 *All actual law is ultimately martial law; and justice is always greater than the law.*

ADULTHOOD

84 Another unhappy result of the pressure economic needs exert on our educational systems is the abrupt way we terminate education at far too young an age. In many parts of the world the great majority leave school for ever with the arrival of puberty. When the age of leisure finally comes to the world we can surely hope that this absurdity will stop.

85 The essential factor in evolutionary survival is self-intelligence. The truest and most valuable recompense that the individual can find in being individual (existing) is the same—self-intelligence.

86 It is difficult to acquire any real self-intelligence before the age of thirty. Part of the joy of being young is that one is on the road to self-knowledge, that one has not arrived at it. Yet we consider that even the best general education should be over by the age of twenty-one.

87 There are three stages of self-indulgence: childhood, adolescence and pre-adulthood (the period between eighteen and thirty). We educate a child out of its myths and its monotonous egocentricity; but fewer and fewer dare to correct the adolescent, and no one dares to correct the pre-adult.

88 Our excessive respect for the pre-adult is partly a relic of the times when the physical energy and strength of that age were of high value in surviving; when killing and running counted; and partly a symptom of our intense longing to be ageless.

89 Each age has its own adulthood. A child can be grownup in its own world. But the more advanced societies now teach their young to be adults when they are still adolescents. Teenagers become adept at mimicking adulthood; and thus many people grown in years are really permanent adolescents mimicking adulthood. Social pressures arrest them at a stage of pseudo-adulthood, and impose on them a mask they first assume to look adult and then wear forever afterwards.

90 *Adulthood is not an age, but a state of knowledge of self.*

ADAM AND EVE

91 The male and female are the two most powerful biological principles; and their smooth inter-action in society is one of the chief signs of social health. In this respect our world shows, in spite of the now general political emancipation of women, considerable sickness; and most of this sickness arises from the selfish tyranny of the male.

92 I interpret the myth of the temptation of Adam in this way. Adam is hatred of change and futile nostalgia for the innocence of animals. The Serpent is imagination, the power to compare, self-consciousness. Eve is the assumption of human responsibility, of the need for progress and the need to control progress. The Garden of Eden is an impossible dream. The Fall is the essential *processus* of evolution. The God of Genesis is a personification of Adam's resentment.

93 Adam is stasis, or conservatism; Eve is kinesis, or

progress. Adam societies are ones in which the man and the father, male gods, exact strict obedience to established institutions and norms of behaviour, as during a majority of the periods of history in our era. The Victorian is a typical such period. Eve societies are those in which the woman and the mother, female gods, encourage innovation and experiment, and fresh definitions, aims, modes of feeling. The Renaissance and our own are typical such ages.

94   There are of course Adam-women and Eve-men; singularly few, among the world's great progressive artists and thinkers, have not belonged to the latter category.

95   The petty, cruel and still prevalent antifeminism of Adam-dominated mankind (the very term 'mankind' is revealing) is the long afterglow of the male's once important physical superiority and greater utility in the battle for survival. To the Adam in man, woman is no more than a rapable receptacle. This male association of femininity with rapability extends far beyond the female body. Progress and innovation are rapable; anything not based on brute power is rapable. All progressive philosophies are feminist. Adam is a princeling in a mountain castle; raids and fortifications, his own power and his own prestige, obsess him.

96   But if Eve had the intelligence to trick Adam out of his foolish dream in the Garden of Eden, she had also the kindness to stick by him afterwards; and it is this aspect of the female principle—tolerance, a general scepticism towards the Adam belief that might is right—that is the most valuable for society. Every mother is an evolutionary system in micro-

cosm; she has no choice but to love what is—her child, ugly or arrogant, criminal or selfish, stupid or deformed. Motherhood is the most fundamental of all trainings in tolerance; and tolerance, as we have still to learn, is the most fundamental of all human wisdoms.

SEXUAL FREEDOM

97 Whatever the professional guardians of public morality say, something more than a mere loss of morality and 'decency' is involved in sex's meteoric advent from behind the curtains and crinolines of Victorian modesty and propriety. It may be a flight from chastity; if right judgement is comparing the present generation with past generations, it is a flight from chastity. But it is also a flight to something.

98 In most societies the unofficial attitude to sexual morality now is that at any rate among unmarried adults there is nothing inherently sinful or criminal about sexual experiences and adventures, whether or not they are accompanied by love, which I will define as the desire to maintain a relationship irrespective of the sexual and, in the final analysis, any other enjoyment to be got from it.

99 Adultery is the disproof of a marriage rather than its betrayal; and divorce is a therapeutic means of purging or ending an unhealthy situation. It no longer in normal circumstances has any moral smell. It is like a visit to an operating theatre. Nature is more likely to be to blame than the individual.

100 But the official attitude, as expressed by churches, newspapers, governments, and in many cases by laws,

is that coitus before and outside marriage is always in some way sinful and anti-social.

101   The social importance we grant to sex lies very much in this forbidden-allowed tension; this deserved-undeserved, this licit-illicit, this private-public, this defiant-submissive, this rebelling-conforming experience. As in all such situations there is plenty of evidence of countersupporting. 'Morality' attacks 'immorality' and gets pleasure and energy from it; 'immorality' tries to defend itself from or to evade 'morality', and gets pleasure and energy from the defence and the evasion.

102   There is of course a fundamental unreality about the official attitude; it is in only a few peripheral areas (such as prostitution and abortion) that its views can be enforced; and if the children know that the farmer can never actually chase them out of most of the orchard with the tempting apples, then of course they have an added inducement to steal them. In any case, we are here dealing with children who would dispute the ownership of the orchard in the first place. We may thus conclude that the opponents of sexual freedom are in fact among its greatest propagators.

103   The result of this ambiguous situation has been the apotheosis of the illicit sexual relationship—illicit, that is, by the standards of official public morality. The time-honoured name for this sort of relationship is the affaire, though the original French phrase (*affaire de coeur*) suggests precisely what the modern puritans complain is lacking. Our affaires now are much more *de corps* than *de coeur*.

104   The dangers of the affaire are well known. Free love does not encourage true love. The emotional insta-

bility that gets one into bed is unlikely to change into the emotional stability one needs when one has to get out. Venereal diseases spread. Neuroses spread. Broken marriages increase, and the innocent children of them suffer, and in their turn breed suffering. It is beyond all these formidable monsters, trackless forests, quagmires, dark nights of the soul, that the Holy Grail, the entirely happy affaire, shines. On the other hand there can be detected in many denunciations of it a pathological dislike of sexual pleasure; and a neutral may well find this kind of 'morality' as prejudiced as the alleged 'bestiality' of the enemy.

105 Sexual attraction and the sexual act are in themselves innocent, neither intrinsically moral nor immoral. Sex is like all great forces: simple a force. We may judge this or that manifestation or situation of the force as moral or immoral; but not the force itself.

106 Coitus is, even at its most animal, the best ritualization of the nature of the whole, of the nature of reality. Part of its mystery is that it has (except as, by current standards, a perversion) to be celebrated in private and learnt in private and enjoyed in private. Part of its pleasure is that it allows infinite variety, both physically and emotionally; in partner and place and mood and manner and time. So the problem may be reduced to this. How can society best allow the individual to experience this profound mystery and variety of pleasure without causing harm?

107 The main sociological argument against the *affaire de corps* is that it instils a natural taste for promiscuity and therefore encourages adultery. This seems more likely to be true than the counter-argument: that it helps in the eventual choice of a husband or wife

and makes a good marriage more probable. This might conceivably be true if young people had the time and the opportunity and the emotional detachment for a wide range of affaires before marriage; but few have. Many such affaires, entered into by psychologically immature and trend-copying young people, lead to disastrous marriages and permanent maladjustments.

108   What in any case is at least as evil as the affaire itself is a situation in which, beckoning in its aura of amoral modernity, it stands as a smart sanctuary, an escape from the pressures of society, as a recompense for having to die, as all sorts of things it partly is but should not essentially be. For in an age where such a relationship still has to be described as officially illicit it is obvious that however innocently it is entered and enjoyed, it will be in conflict with all those unpermissive modes of thought and conscience, the communal superego, that society has had us taught.

109   Most adolescents and pre-adults are naturally confused by two drives that mimic each other: the drive towards sexual experience (in itself part of a deeper drive towards the hazardous and adventurous) and the drive towards love as institutionalized in marriage (in itself part of the drive towards certainty and security). They find it difficult to separate the two; what starts as one can in even a few moments become the other. A desire to kiss becomes the desire to live together for a lifetime, the decision to marry becomes the abrupt yearning for another body.

110   Much more of the sexual education of adolescents should be devoted to teaching them the aetiology of love; this is just as important as the physiology of coitus.

111 There is a widespread belief that love and sex are incompatible. That if you have considerable sexual experience you cannot love (Don Juan); and that if you love (maintain a permanent relationship like marriage) you will sooner or later cease to enjoy sex. The belief is strengthened by the regarding of marriage as a mere licensing of sex instead of as an affirmation of love. If you sternly forbid the affaire to the unmarried, you must not expect them to understand marriage for what it should be: the intention to love, not the desire to enjoy coitus licitly.

112 The charm of the illicit sexual experience is sometimes almost as much that it is illicit as that it is sexual. When Meaulnes eventually refound his *domaine perdu, domaine sans nom,* when at last he met the mysterious Yvonne de Galais again, what did he do? He ran away after the very first night of their marriage.*

113 When the individual is being attacked on all sides by the forces of anti-individuality; by the nemo; by the sense that death is absolute, by the dehumanizing processes of both mass production and mass producing: the affaire represents not only an escape into the enchanted garden of the ego but also a quasi-heroic gesture of human defiance.

114 Just as art is being used by the individual as an outlet for the resentments caused by the inadequacies of society, so is the affaire. It is a day spent playing truant from an excruciatingly dull and wintry school. The whole of contemporary popular art is based on this notion. Listen to the lyrics of 'pop' music. Compare the sexuality of a figure like James Bond with that of figures like Maigret or Sherlock Holmes.

115 The same can be said for advertising. Cigarettes are not recommended for their quality as cigarettes but as the right accompaniment to the affaire; recipients, the advertisers say, can be 'won', 'seduced', 'enchanted' (shades of the love philtre) by all sorts of innocent objects—chocolates, pens, jewelry, packaged holidays, and the rest. Similar tendencies can be seen in much car and clothing advertising, though here the appeal is that of the aphrodisiac rather than of the love philtre. This car makes a man more virile; this dress suggests a Messalina. Even fabrics have moral associations woven into them by the publicity men. You no longer buy black leather, you buy its suggestions of sadistic perversion.

116 The extramarital affaire becomes particularly siren-like after several years of marriage. There is among husbands a kind of *nostalgie de la vierge,* among wives a longing for a life outside the domestic prison, those grim four walls constituted by husband, children, housework and kitchen. In men the desire seems to be directly sexual. In women it may be a more complex longing. But in both cases it is a flight from reality; and if children are involved, a flight from responsibility.*

117 For the would-be adulterous husband or wife the pressures to enter into an affaire may be less, and the penalties greater, than they are for the unmarried person. The moral issue is generally much clearer; but other factors, such as the sharper sense of failure or dissatisfaction that age brings, the memory of pre-marital affaires (or the memory of the lack of them), the monotony of marriage and the general climate of a society intoxicated by permissivity, may make the objectively clear issue subjectively harder to see now than ever before in history.

118 Pleasure may come to seem a responsibility; while responsibility may rarely come to seem what it can be, a pleasure. How many marriages break because so many marriages break?

119 When the whole philosophy of a capitalist society can be reduced to this: You owe yourself as much as you can get, whether it be in money, in status, in possessions, in enjoyments, or in experiences. Can pleasure not become a duty?

120 The tendency of any capitalist society is to turn all experiences and relationships into objects, objects that can be assessed on the same scale of values as washing machines and central heating, that is, by the comparative cheapness of the utility and pleasurability to be derived from it. Furthermore, the tendency in an overpopulated and inflation-fearing society is to make things expendable, and therefore to make expendability a virtue and pleasure. Throw the old object away and get a new. As we are haunted by the affaire, so are we haunted by the pursuit of the new, and these ghosts are brothers.

121 Fathers and mothers no longer see their children as children; as they grow they see them increasingly as rivals in the enjoyment race. What is more, rivals who seem bound to win. However harmless it is, whenever a change of social habits brings more pleasure into the world, some older people will object, simply because they had to do without the change when they were young, and others will frantically and foolishly try to catch up. It is not just chastity, morality and marriage that are under attack, but the whole traditional concept of what we are and what we are for.

122 Some suggest that we are moving into an age when it will be considered normal that one should have sexual relationships as one wants and with whom one wants, regardless of other social ties. They say this will be possible because copulation will come to seem no more significant than dancing or conversing as one wants or with whom one wants. In such a society there would be nothing exceptionable about coitus in public; and the queues that now form to see Fonteyn and Nureyev would form to see skilled practitioners in an even older art. We should, in short, have returned to ancient pre-Christian ideas of sex as an activity that does not require any special privacy, nor evoke any special inhibitions. It is dimly possible that this depuritanization of sex will one day take place; but for as long as the present sexual conventions, licit and illicit, supply some deeper need of man in an unsatisfying society, it will not.

123 In an education in humanity the teaching on this matter must surely be based on the following considerations:

(A) One great argument for more teaching of self-analysis, and for more analysis of the self in general, is that half the pain caused by the affaire and the broken marriage, and the very causing itself, is due to the ignorance of each of both each and the other.

(B) The excessive commercialization of sex, and especially of the affaire, is not the brightest jewel in capitalism's crown.

(C) Of all activities, sex is the least amenable to general judgements. It is always relative, always situational. It is as silly to proscribe it as to prescribe it. All that can be done is to educate about it.

(D) To teach the physiology of sex without the psychology of love is to teach all about a ship except how to steer it.

(E) Spokesmen for 'morality' have no right to condemn or to try to prevent any kind of sexual relationship unless they can demonstrate that it is bringing society more unhappiness than happiness. It is always easy to produce illegitimacy, divorce, and veneral disease statistics; but the statistics of sexual happiness are harder to come by.

(F) A child is a law against adultery; and though an adulterer can no longer break the law, he can still break the child. But as children grow, divorce becomes less and less a crime, since the disharmony the growing child increasingly takes note of may do as much harm as the ending of the marriage.

(G) Just as surgery can be abused, so can divorce. But that a thing can be abused is never an argument against it.

(H) The noblest relationship is marriage, that is, love. Its nobility resides in its altruism, the desire to serve another beyond all the pleasures of the relationship; and in its refusal ever to regard the other as a thing, an object, a utilizability.

(I) Sex is an exchange of pleasures, of needs; love is a giving without return.

(J) It is this giving without return, this helping without reward, this surplus of pure good, that identifies the uniqueness of man as well as the true nature of the true marriage. This is the quintessence the great alchemy of sex is for; and every adultery adulterates it, every infidelity betrays it, every cruelty clouds it.

THE INWARD EDUCATION

124 Man should not be, above all, necessary to society; he should be above all necessary to himself. He is not educated until his self has been analysed and he un-

derstands the common psychological mechanisms. At present we teach the persona, not the real self. The persona is made up of all the incrustations, however formed, that hide what I really feel and what I really think. It is plain that we must all have some persona; but not that we should hide so much of our real selves as our societies and their educational systems now require. We must not teach how to conform (society does that automatically) but how and when not to conform.*

THE IMPORTANCE OF THE NOW

125   In this universe of mirrors and metaphors, man reflects and parallels all the realities. They are all in each mind, but deep. The infinite process is made finite in each thing; each thing is a cross section of eternity.

126   The end of all evolution is dissolution. This is not absurd. It would be absurd if the end of evolution was the perfect state. It would be absurd if evolution had any other end but dissolution. Evolution is therefore meaningless if it is evolution towards. It is now or nothing. A better state, a better design, a better self, a better world; but always these things beginning now.

127   The whole is not a chain, but a spinning top. The top spins on, but stays in one place. One can point to a link in the chain or a point on the road and say 'That is the best place to be'; but a top is always in the same place. The weight of the top must be distributed evenly about its central axis, or the top will tilt and wobble. All those tendencies, in so many

religious and political philosophies, to think and persuade away from the present life, from the now; those attempts to make us put the great weight and energy of our beliefs and hopes in some other world (heavenly or utopian) are like erratic movements of weight inside the top. We disperse our powers centrifugally. The real meaning of life is close around the axis of each now.

128 It is not by accident that the discovery of self is not encouraged by the state. An educational system is organized by the state to prolong the state; and the discovery of the self is also often the discovery of what the state really is.

129 Our present educational systems are all paramilitary. Their aim is to produce servants or soldiers who obey without question and who accept their training as the best possible training. Those who are most successful in a state are those who have most interest in prolonging the state as it is; they are also those who have most to say in the educational system, and in particular by ensuring that the educational product they want is the most highly rewarded.

130 State and government are ways of thinking of the then; they are systems of the then. We say 'He lives in the past' and we say it with pity or contempt; yet most of us live in the future.

131 The state does not want to be; it wants to survive.

132 It is true that many of us live in tomorrow because today is uninhabitable. But to make today habitable is not in the interest of the state. It is principally the inadequacies of the state that force man to live in the

future; and the main reason for these inadequacies is that the states of the world refuse to act jointly and do these two essential things—depopulate and educate.

INWARD KNOWLEDGE

133 Most of us still carry in our minds the myth of a clearly marked frontier between the healthy and the sick; and perhaps in no area so much as mental health, which happens to be the area where such demarcations are most absurd. The endless fun made of psychiatry, and especially of psycho-analysis, is a sure sign of fear. The 'healthy' among us tend to cherish our phobias and neuroses; we do not want them exposed.

134 There is no greater inadequacy in our present systems of education than the attitude to psychology. The notion that school psychologists should devote all their time to the 'sick' (the neurotic or backward students) is absurd. The 'healthy' need their attention just as much. A key subject in any education in humanity must be general psychology; and a key service must be the personal analysis of each student.

135 This is not the place to discuss the comparative merits of the different schools of psychological theory. But since the psychological aspect of an education in humanity must have a strong social bias, we should certainly pay far more attention to the biological theory of domination-subordinance.

136 This theory has sprung from the study of non-human primates like gorillas and chimpanzees. It has been discovered that their relative domination over or sub-

ordinance to one another depends largely on size and (outside the periods when females are in heat) non-sexual factors akin to human self-confidence. Thus a large female and a small male in the same cage will be respectively the dominator and the subordinate; the male will 'present' (adopt female copulatory positions) as a sign of submission. We must realize that all humans adopt (or veer between) one or other of these roles, *irrespective of sex*. The common organizational behaviour known as boot- or arse-licking is a clear example of the subordinate role. The man who goes in for it is metaphorically 'pre-senting'; and it is not for nothing that the two com-monest obscenities in every language are 'Fuck you' and 'Bugger you'. They are both assertions about dominance, and the nature of the dominated.

137 But of course human beings are not caged and live in far more complex situations; and it is the chain-reaction aspect of this relationship need that is the most dangerous for society. The conscious subordi-nate in regard to one person will become the more or less aggrieved dominant in regard to another. Human subordinates are generally conscious of their subordination, and the secret displeasures it brings them, and so the road to a compensatory pleasure elsewhere in their lives becomes only too clearly sign-posted. The general 'historical resentment' or sense of inferiority felt by the German people between the two world wars leads straight to the persecution of the Jews. The vicious circle of sado-masochism in society is only too easily and naturally established.

138 Birds provide us with the clearest example of the mechanism nature has evolved to deal with this vicious circle—that is, 'territory'. In some species, the biological value of nesting in large colonies is so

great that their sense of territory is small; and in these species we find highly developed systems of pecking-order. Such species gain both ways. They are defended by sheer numbers; and the ones who get pecked to death are the weakest individuals. Other species, at any rate during the breeding season, establish areas on which no other pair may trespass with impunity. Under this system they are less prone to infectious disease, famine, and so on. That both systems work we may see clearly in the Corvidae (the most 'intelligent' bird family) in which closely-related species have adopted different systems. Thus jackdaws and rooks live largely communally; while crows and magpies live largely in pairs or small families.

139 Man utilizes both systems. We defend ourselves and organize our essential needs communally; and it is in these communal situations, which obviously require hierarchies of command and importance, that we see most clearly the workings of the human pecking-order. But we equally demand domains analogous to the territories of the solitary species, in which we can be the dominants. Though we more naturally think of spheres like the home, the garden, the property and possessions we own, as our 'territory', we all carry about with us a much more important psychological corpus of emotions and ideas and beliefs. This *mental territory* governs all our social behaviour, and it is of vital importance that it receives more study and attention in our education, since it is almost certainly the aspect of ourselves that we know least of.

140 A very frequent demarcator of this mental territory is the Jungian complex. A complex is an idea or group of associated ideas about which we cannot

think rationally and objectively, but only emotionally and subjectively. Jungian theory explains the complex as the conscious manifestation of unconscious fears and desires; but complexes also serve very well as warnings to other members of the species not to trespass in this area. A crank who maintains that the world is flat may become very angry when he is given clear proofs to the contrary. His anger will certainly not prove his case; but it will often tend to preserve his case from further attack.

141 The prime intention of this mental territory we erect around us is of course to counteract our sense of nemo, of nonentity; and this immediately warns us that it is not sufficient to destroy the vanities, illusions and complexes with which we wall ourselves in (or demarcate ourselves) since thereby we risk destroying identity. What we need to do is to discover what is valid in this demarcation-fortification material; and then to let the discovery of what is valid show to the frightened person inside the fortifications what is invalid.

142 The understanding of the roles subordinance and domination play in our lives; the analysis of what is strictly necessary in the role adopted (or of the way the individual distributes different roles to himself); and establishing the validity of the mental territory we attempt to define; these represent the basis for an educational personal analysis of each student. This does not of course preclude analysis based on more familiar psychological theories; the systems of Adler and Karen Horney must be particularly relevant. But this gives most hope of bringing more self-understanding, tolerance and a greater equality in existence to our world.*

143 I can best describe this inward phase of education by giving the questions it should, by the time it is complete, enable its students to answer.

Who am I?

In what ways am I similar to and in what ways different from most other human beings?

What are my duties to myself?

What are my duties towards others?

What are the duties of an employer, an employee, a member of a state, an individual?

To what extent, given my capacities, do I fulfil and balance these conflicting extremes?

What do I mean by love?

What do I mean by guilt?

What do I mean by justice?

What is science to me?

What is art to me?

THE SYNOPTIC EDUCATION

144 This education is concerned with only one thing: why all is as all is. Since we are in the same situation as human beings, it must be identical the world over.

145 It must comprehend the study of the great religions and philosophies of the past—and present—but since its intention is synoptic, they must be presented as interpretations or metaphors of reality. We know that in this domain the truth is always more complex than our formulation of it.

146 It seems to me that the inescapable conclusion of any truly synoptic view of human existence is that the chief aim of evolution is the preservation of matter. Each form of animate matter is given a reason for living; and our human reason is the establishment of

equality of recompense in living. Since in our present world unnecessary inequalities are ubiquitous, a proper synoptic education must lead to a sense of discontent that is also a sense of moral purpose.

147 I believe also that it must discredit the notion that God (in the traditional sense) can, in any but the negative way I have described, be presumed to have human characteristics or powers; in short, we will do better to assume there is no such God.

148 Finally it will destroy our last childish belief in an afterlife, through which, like a hole in a bucket, real life leaks away. If death is absolute, life is absolute; life is sacred; kindness to other life is essential; today is more than tomorrow; noon conquers night. To do is now, living; death is never able to do.

149 Everything finally is means, nothing is end. All we call immortal is mortal. What a nuclear holocaust may do, time certainly will do. So live now, and teach it.

150 The mystery is not in the beginning or the end, but in the now. There was no beginning; there will be no end.

10

THE IMPORTANCE OF ART

1 By art, I mean all the arts; by artists, creators in all the arts; by artefacts, anything that can be enjoyed in the absence of the artist. Since the discovery of sound recording and cinematography it is arguable that great performances, for example in music or in drama, are now artefacts. However, by artefact I mean here what it traditionally means. The composer's, not the interpretant's, kind of creating; the playwright's, not the actor's.

2 The practice and experience of art is as important to man as the use and knowledge of science. These two great manners of apprehending and enjoying existence are complementary, not hostile. The specific value of art for man is that it is closer to reality than science; that it is not dominated, as science must be, by logic and reason; that it is therefore essentially a liberating activity, while science—for excellent and necessary causes—is a constricting one. Finally and most importantly it is the best, because richest, most complex and most easily comprehensible, medium of communication between human beings.

TIME AND ART

3 Art best conquers time, and therefore the nemo. It constitutes that timeless world of the full intellect (Teilhard du Chardin's noösphere) where each arte-

fact is contemporary, and as nearly immortal as an object in a cosmos without immortality can be.*

4 We enter the noösphere by creating, whereby we constitute it, or by experiencing, whereby we exist in it. Both functions are in communion; 'actors' and 'audience', 'celebrants' and 'congregation'. For experiencing art is experiencing, among other things, that others have existed as we exist, and still exist in this creation of their existing.

5 The noösphere is equally created, of course, by great achievements in science. But the important distinction between the artefact and what we may call the scientifact is that the former, unlike the latter, can never be proved wrong. An artefact, however poor artistically, is an object in a context where proof and disproof do not exist. This is why the artefact is so much more resistant to time; the cosmogonies of ancient Mesopotamia make very little impression and have very little interest for us. They are disproved scientifacts. On the other hand the artefacts of ancient Mesopotamia retain both interest and immediacy. The great test of a scientifact is its utility *now;* of course utility-now is of vital importance to us and explains the priority we accord science in our world now. But disproved scientifacts—those that no longer have this utility—become mere items of interest in the history of science and the development of the human mind, items that we tend to judge by increasingly aesthetic standards; for their neatness of exposition, style, form and so forth. They become, in fact, disguised artefacts, though far less free of time and therefore less immediate and important to us than true artefacts.

6 This timelessness of the artefact has a quantitative

aspect; it is of course illogical and ungrammatical to speak of one object as being more timeless than another. But our eagerness to conquer time—or to see time conquered—does lead us into this illogic. We have to be very ruthless, suppress all our intuitive feeling, to find worthless ugliness in an artefact of over a few hundred years' age. It is true that the passage of time often constitutes a kind of selection committee; objects of beauty stand a better chance of being preserved than ugly ones. But in many cases —such as archaeological finds—we know that there was no selection committee. Ugly objects in their own age survive side by side with beautiful ones; and yet we find beauty in them all.

7 Time, the length of survival of an artefact, becomes a factor in its beauty. The aesthetic value of the object becomes confused with its value as witness, or carrier of information from far places. Its beauty merges into its usefulness as a piece of human communication; and this will plainly vary according to our need of (previous lack of) communication from the particular source.

8 The older an artefact the nearer it is to the timeless; the newer the artefact the further away. Because it is new, yearless, it has none of the beauty or utility of having survived in time; but it may have the beauty or utility of being likely to survive time. Some artefacts are likely to survive because the future can use them as evidence against the age that produced them; and others as evidence for. Official art requires only the second kind. Monuments, not testaments.

9 Though this prejudice in favour of what is old or likely to become old affects our judgement of artefacts, and even our attitude to such things as fossils,

it does not normally affect our judgement of other objects. In the stone, the mere enduringness of matter; in the artefact, the enduringness of man; of a name or of a nameless human existence; the thumbmark below the handle of this Minoan pot.

10 An aged artefact is both what could not be created today and what still exists today; we admire in it the number of nows survived. It is doubly present; both survivant and now. This explains the long vogue of the antique. As organisms aware that we shall die, we are in one way nearer the oldest artefact than the newest natural object.

11 Since the normal standard by which we judge artefacts is their worthiness to survive, it is only to be expected that a contrary kind of artefact should on occasion appeal to us: that is, the ephemeral artefact.

12 A whole host of minor arts are, in themselves and by their natures, banned from the noösphere: for example, the arts of gardening, coiffure, *haute cuisine*, pyrotechnics. If they get into the noösphere, it is by chance, by happening to be made items in some greater art. It is true that the camera and the cine-camera, the tape recorder and the tin can, counter the intrinsic ephemerality of these sub-arts; and it is sometimes possible to reconstitute them by recipe. But it is precisely a part of our pleasure that the direct experience of these arts is essentially ephemeral and not shared by others.

13 The parallel with man: we also pass like fireworks, like flowers, like fine food and fine wine. We feel a kinship with these ephemeral arts, these manifestations of human skill that are born after and die before us; that may be come and gone in a few seconds.

Unrecorded performances in music, on the stage and on the sports field fall into the same category.

14 So there are two kinds of artefact: those we admire, and perhaps envy, because they survive us and those we like, and perhaps pity, because they do not. Both kinds are aspects of feeling about time.

15 All art both generalizes and particularizes; that is, tries to flower in all time, but is rooted in one time. An archaic statue, an abstract painting, a twelve-tone sequence may mainly generalize (all time); a Holbein portrait, a *haiku,* a flamenco song may mainly particularize (one time). But in the portrait of Ann Cresacre by Holbein I see one sixteenth-century woman and yet all young women of a certain kind; in this austere and totally unrooted concatenation of notes by Webern I hear nonetheless the expression of one particular early twentieth-century mind.

16 This balance between particularization and generalization that the artist struggles to achieve, nature achieves without struggle. This butterfly is unique and universal; it is both itself and exactly like any other butterfly of its species. This nightingale sings to me as it sang to my grandfather, and his grandfather; and to Homer's grandfather; it is the same nightingale and not the same nightingale. It is now and it is ever. Through the voice I hear—and Keats heard—this passing night I enter reality two ways; and at the centre meet my richer self.

17 How we see a natural object depends on us— whether we see it vertically, in this one moment, now, or horizontally, in all its past; or both together; and so in art we try to say both in the one statement. Always these complex factors of time are inherent in the seeing and the saying.

18 How I see this artefact may depend on how the artist
wants me to see it, vertically-now or horizontally-
ever; but even with artefacts I can choose. I can see
Caravaggio's *St Jerome* vertically-now, in itself, or
horizontally-ever, inserted in the history of painting.
I can see it as a portrait of one old man, or as a study
of the hermit; as a quasi-academic study in chiaro-
scuro problems; as a document with information
about Caravaggio himself, about his age; and so on.

19 We also experience artefacts in 'intended' and 'fortuitous' ways (see group 5, note 49) and in 'objective'
and 'actual' ones (6.23). These too are aspects of
time.

20 Both in the creator and the spectator, art is the attempt to transcend time. Whatever else it may be
and intend, an artefact is always a nexus of human
feelings about time; and it is no coincidence that our
current preoccupation with art comes at the same
time as our new realization of the shortness of our
duration in infinity.

THE ARTIST AND HIS ART

21 Inside this fundamental relationship with time, the
artist has used his art, his ability to create, for three
main purposes; and he has two main tests of success.

22 His simplest purpose is to describe the outer world;
his next is to express his feelings about that outer
world, and his last is to express his feelings about
himself. Whichever of these purposes he has in mind,
his test may be that he satisfies himself or it may be
that he satisfies and pleases others. It is probable that
all three purposes are present, and both tests satisfied,
in varying degrees in almost every artefact. The sim-

plest and most unemotional realism, mere description, still involves the selection of the object described; any expression of feeling about the outer world must obviously also be an expression of the artist's inner world; and there can be few artists so self-sure that the approval of others means nothing to them. For all that, there have been great shifts in emphasis during the last two hundred years.

23 When other means of description were almost non-existent, art had a great representational and descriptive duty. It made what was absent present; the bison loomed on the cave wall. The, to our eyes, charming stylization of Stone Age art was certainly, to begin with, a result of technical inefficiency, not of lack of desire to paint as realistically as possible. But very early on the cave men must have realized that styliza-tion had a double charm: it not only brought to mind and recorded the past or the absent, but the devi-ations from strict reality also kept the real past and the real pressure at bay. So the first function of art and stylization was probably magic: to distance reality at the same time as it was invoked.

24 There was also a strong ritual motive in the use of stylization. It was only a short step from drawing animals in charcoal in order to give information to accentuating certain features because such accentua-tion seemed more likely to guarantee the end desired —killing for food, and so on. Some scientists argue that this ritual-traditional element in art represents a great flaw in its utility, a kind of only partially sloughed skin the poor artist has to drag behind him. They point to all the empirical methods and criteria that science has evolved to rid itself of ritual-tradi-tional elements. But this is akin to the absurd fallacy that one can produce great art by the exercise of pure

logic and pure reason. Art springs from humanity as it is, from history, from time, and it is always more complex in statement, if not in method, than science. It is for other human beings; it is consolatory or menacing, but always more or less therapeutic in intention, and its therapy has to apply to a thing far too complex (and indeed ritualistic) for science to control or cure—the human mind.

25 A second great utility of style must have become more or less consciously apparent to the visual artists of primitive man. Style distorts reality. But this distortion is in fact art's most vital tool, since by its use the artist is enabled to express his own or communal feelings and aspirations. Fifty-breasted fertility goddesses are clearly not failures to portray realistically, but visual translations of feeling. The parallel in language is the development of metaphor and all that goes beyond the strict needs of communication. The parallel in music is the development of all those elements that are not strictly necessary as accompaniment to dancing; all beyond the drum or clapped hands.

26 The first two artistic purposes, representational and outer-feeling, were the main ones until at least the Renaissance; and the third purpose, inner-feeling, has been triumphant only during the last century or so. There are two principal reasons for this. The first is that the development of better means of exact representation than art has made purely descriptive realistic art seem largely mischanneled. The camera, the tape recorder, the development of technical vocabularies and scientific methods of linguistic observation— these things all make much overtly representational art look feeble and foolish. That we are not more aware of this is probably due to the fact that historically this representational art is of great value to

us, and we still have not shaken off the habit of using it, even though far better means are now at hand.

27 If for example we really want to honour an eminent man it would surely be better to have good photographs or films of him taken, or to publish linguistic accounts of his eminence; anything rather than having his portrait painted by some 'academic' hack. No one supposes such portraits have any intrinsic biographical or artistic merit; they merely satisfy a traditional social convention about the rewards of eminence.

28 The second reason for the triumph of inner-feeling art is the rise of the importance of self in the existence of each as a result of those nemo-creating conditions I have already mentioned. It is not coincidence that the Romantic Movement, whose influence is still so powerful, was a result of the machine-orientated Industrial Revolution; and many of our contemporary artistic problems spring from a similar hostile polarity.

29 The result of this has inevitably been the emergence of style as the principal gauge of artistic worth. Content has never seemed less important; and we may see the history of the arts since the Renaissance (the last period in which content was at least conceded equal status) as the slow but now almost total triumph of the means of expression over the thing expressed.

30 A symptom of this triumph is the attitude of artists to the signing of artefacts. It is with the Greeks that signing becomes frequent, and as one would expect, it is in the most self-conscious art, literature, that it was commonest. But as late as the Renaissance many artists felt no great need to sign; and even today there is a tradition of anonymity in those craft arts, like

pottery and furniture-making, that are least susceptible of exploitation by the artist's self.

31 The artist's main need today seems to him to be the expression of his signed feelings about himself and his world; and as our need for representational art has dwindled, so have arisen all those modes and styles, like abstractionism and atonalism and dadaism, that put a very low value on exact representation of the outer world (craft qualities) and on past conventions about the artist's duty to that world; but that conversely allow the widest possible field for the expression of an unmistakably unique self. The enormous 'liberation' in style and technique and instrumentation (use of materials) that has taken place in our century is strictly caused by the need artists have felt for creative *Lebensraum;* in short, by their sense of imprisonment in the mass of other artists. Prison destroys personal identity; and this is what the artist now most fears.

32 But if the main concern of art becomes to express individuality, the audience must seem to the artist less important; and the slighted audience will in turn reject this doubly selfish art, especially when all other artistic purposes are so excluded that the artefacts must appear hermetic to anyone without special information about the artist's intentions.

33 Two characteristic camps will emerge, and have emerged: one of artists who pursue their own feelings and their own self-satisfaction and who expect their audiences to come to them out of a sense of duty toward 'pure' or 'sincere' art; and the other of artists who exploit the desire of the audience to be wooed, amused and entertained. There is nothing new in this

situation. But the camps have never been so clearly defined and so antagonistic.

34 All inner-feeling art thus becomes a disguised form of the self-portrait. Everywhere the artist sees himself as in a mirror. The craft of the art suffers; craftsmanship even becomes 'insincere' and 'commercial'. Even worse, in order to conceal the triviality, banality or illogic of his inner self, the artist may introduce deliberately hermetic and ambiguous elements into his art. This is more easily done in painting and music than in literature, because the word is a more precise symbol and false ambiguity and hermeticism are in general more easily detectable in literature than in the other arts.

ART AND SOCIETY

35 But the tyranny of self-expresion is not the only factor the modern artist has to contend with. One of the most striking characteristics of our age has been the ubiquitous use of the poles of violence, cruelty, evil, insecurity, perversion, confusion, ambiguity, iconoclasm and anarchy in popular and intellectual entertainment and art. The happy end becomes 'sentimental'; the open or tragic ends become 'real'. It is often said that art movements do no more than reflect those of history. Our century is evidently violent, cruel, and all the rest: so what else should its arts be if not black?

36 But this suggests that the artist is incapable of any higher aspiration than that of presenting a mirror to the world around him. This is not to deny that a great deal of the 'black' art of our time is, alas, historically justifiable; but it is very often a result of the pressures unfairly put upon art by society. The artist creates

blackly because society expects him to; not because he essentially wants to.

37 Black art may bring us a certain kind of pleasure, not only because we are secretly violent, cruel and nihilistically chaotic ourselves, and not only because the emotions such art arouses afford a vivid contrast to our day-by-day lives in a safe society, but because those grey-fearing lives gain a reality, colour and validity they lack if they have no such contrast easily accessible to them. This violent death is my safe life; this distorted shape is my symmetry; this meaningless poem is my clear meaning.

38 One of the deepest pleasures of tragedy is simply that we survive it; the tragedy might have, but has not, happened to us. We not only experience the tragedy empathetically; we have the subsequent survival.

39 There is thus a very deep-rooted sense in which the public never takes 'black' art at its face value. It is indeed a frequent defence of pornography that whatever its apparent intentions, its final effects are often highly moral. The spectacle of 'vice' and perversion serves to remind people of their own virtues and their normality. Sadism is far more likely to provoke increased respect for others than further sadism; and so on. But whichever view one takes—that such art corrupts society or that it secretly benefits it—the effect on the artist must be bad.

40 Art has to provide today what ignorance and social and physical conditions provided in the past: insecurity, violence and hazard. This is a perversion of its true function.

41 It is this unnatural role that accounts for a particu-

larly common manifestation of guilty conscience among many so-called avant-garde artists; the attempt to suppress the creator from the creation, to reduce the artefact to the status of a game with as few rules as possible. Paintings where the colours and the shapes and the textures are a matter of hazard; music where the amount of improvisation demanded of the players reduces the composer to a cipher; novels and poems where the arrangement of words or pages is purely fortuitous. The scientific basis for this aleatory art is perhaps the famous, and famously misunderstood, principle of indeterminacy; and it also springs from a totally mistaken notion that the absence of an intervening, in our everyday sense of intervening, God means that existence is meaningless. Such art is, though apparently self-effacing, absurdly arrogant.*

42 An artist can choose not to be an artist, but he cannot be an artist who has chosen not to be an artist.

ARTISTS AND NON-ARTISTS

43 The artistic experience, from the late eighteenth century onwards, usurps the religious experience. Just as the medieval church was full of priests who should have been artists, so our age is filled with artists who would once have been priests.

44 Many modern artists would no doubt dispute that they are priests *manqués*. That is because they have substituted the pursuit of artistic 'truth' for the pursuit of good. There was so much injustice on every doorstep, once; it was easy to know what good meant in terms of action. But now even in didactic art the pursuit is much more of the right aesthetic or artistic expression of the moral than of the moral itself.

45 It is true that the best right expression of the moral best serves the moral; the style is the thought. But an excessive pre-occupation with the style of the thought tends to produce a devaluation of the thought: just as many priests became so pre-occupied with ritual and the presentation of doctrine that they forgot the true nature of the priesthood, so have many artists become so blind to all but the requirements of style that they have lost all sight of, or pay no more than lip service to, any human moral content. Morality becomes a kind of ability to convey.

46 The growth of industrial civilization, the stereotyped work processes, the population surge, the realization, in an age of close international communication, that men are psychologically more similar than different: all these factors drive the individual to the individual-izing act, the act of artistic creation: and above all to the creation that expresses self. Drink, drugs, prom-iscuity, unkemptness, the notorious conventions of anticonvention, are explicable statistically as well as emotionally.

47 The ominous innumerability of our world, the endless repetition of triviality, breeds the nemo. Our modern saints are the damned: the Soutines and the Alban Bergs, the Rilkes and the Rimbauds, the Dylan Thomases and the Scott Fitzgeralds, the Jean Harlows and the Marilyn Monroes. They are to us what the martyrs were to the early church; that is, they all died for the worthiest of causes—immortality of name.

48 How else can we explain the popularity of romanced biographies of artists and cheap biographical films? These new hagiographies, like the old ones, are less concerned with the ultimate achievements and mo-tives of their subjects than with the outward and

sensational facts of their private lives. Van Gogh with a razor in his hand; not with a brush.

49 But this produces an imitative insincerity in many modern artists. The great artists who have gone to the dark poles have been driven there. They are always looking back towards the light. They have fallen. Their imitators did not fall; they jumped down.

50 The lives of 'bohemian' artists, of *les grands maudits,* are more interesting to the public than their works. They know they could never make the works; but they might have lived the life.

51 Increasingly art has to express what the nonscientific intellectual *élite* of the world think and feel; it is for the top of the pyramid, the literate few. When the chief fields for intellectual expression and the main channels for the stating of personal views of life were theology and philosophy, the artist was able to remain in closer contact with a public. But now that art has become the chief mode of stating self, now that the theologian-philosopher is metamorphosed into the artist, an enormous gap has sprung.

52 The only persons who might have stopped this schism between the artist and the non-artist are the critics. But the more obscure and the more ambiguous a work of art the more need there is of interpretation and interpreters. There are thus excellent professional reasons for critics to encourage the schism. There is also a marked tendency to lycanthropism: to being a creator by day and a critic by night.*

53 Our society requires the artist to live like this, and to present an image like this, just as by its tedium and its conformity it obliges him to create 'black' art and

entertainment. From the point of view of society, the artist thus dictated to and obeying the dictate is fulfilling a useful function. But my belief is that such a function is not the function of art.

54 The true *primary* function of art is not to remedy the faults and deficiencies of society, to provide salt for the ordinary; but in conjunction with science to occupy the cestral position in human existence.

55 Because in general we approach the arts and entertainment from outside, because we *go* to art, we regard it as external to the main part of our life. We go to the theatre, to the cinema, the opera, the ballet; to museums; to sports fields (for a part of all great games is as much art as theatre or ballet). Even our reading is outside the main occupations of our day; and even the art that is piped into our homes we feel comes from outside. This holding at a distance of art, this constant spectatoring, is thoroughly evil.

56 Another factor, the now ubiquitous availability of reproductions of art, aggravates matters; less and less do ordinary people have any *direct* contact with either artists or their creations. Records and radio usurp the experience of live music, 'replicas' and magazine articles the experience of the actual painting. It may seem that literature at least cannot be experienced at a remove in this way; but increasingly people prefer to absorb novels in the form of television plays or films—and the same goes for theatre plays. Only the poem seems of its nature sacrosanct; and we may wonder if this is not precisely why poetry has become such a minority art in our time.

57 If we consign art to the leisure outprovinces of our lives, and even there experience it mostly in some

indirect form, it becomes a mere aspect of good living
—that is, a matter of facts, not feeling; of placing, of
showing off cultural knowledge; of identifying and
collecting. In short, it produces a total inability to see
things in themselves, but an obsessional need to place
them in a social, snobbish or voguish context. The
vogue (that is, the new style) becomes an aspect
of the general social-economic need for quick expendability.

58 This too, and perhaps most strikingly, corrupts the
artist. And it has brought about the highly rococo
atmosphere in which the contemporary arts now
languish. The great eighteenth-century rococo arts
were the visual and aural ones; the style was characterized by great facility, a desire to charm the bored
and jaded palate, to amuse by decoration rather than
by content—indeed serious content was eschewed.
We see all these old tricks writ new in our modern
arts, with their brilliantly pointless dialogues, their
vivid descriptions of things not worth describing,
their elegant vacuity, their fascination with the synthetic and their distaste for the natural.

59 The modern world and modern sensibilities are increasingly complex; but it is not the function of the
artist to complicate the complexities; if anything, it
should be to unravel them. For many nowadays what
is taken as a criterion is not the meaning, but a skill
in hinting at meanings. Any good computer will beat
man at this.

THE GENIUS AND THE CRAFTSMAN

60 The concept of the genius arose, as we might expect,
with the Romantic Movement; since that movement

was above all a revolt of the individual against the machine in all its forms (including reason), it was inevitable that the super-individual—the Napoleon, the Beethoven, the Goethe—should be adulated.

61 The artefacts of a genius are distinguished by rich human content, for which he forges new images and new techniques, creates new styles. He sees himself as a unique eruption in the desert of the banal. He feels himself mysteriously inspired or possessed. The craftsman, on the other hand, is content to use the traditional materials and techniques. The more self-possessed he is, the better craftsman he will be. What pleases him is skill of execution. He is very concerned with his contemporary success, his market value. If a certain kind of social or political commitment is fashionable, he may be committed; but out of fashion, not conviction. The genius, of course, is largely indifferent to contemporary success; and his commitment to his ideals, both artistic and political, is profoundly, Byronically, indifferent to their contemporary popularity.

62 We can all see that being a genius constitutes a very good recipe for defeating the sense of nemo; and that is why the vast majority of modern artists want tacitly to be geniuses rather than craftsmen. It may be clear to the discriminating critic, it may even be clear to them themselves, that they are not geniuses; but the public in general is very inclined to take artists at their own valuation. We thus arrive at a situation in which all experiment is considered admirable (and the discovery of new techniques and materials is an act of genius in itself, regardless of the fact that all true genius has been driven to such discoveries by the need to express some new *content*) and all craftmanship 'academic' and more or less despicable.

63 Of course our real geniuses are indispensable to us and to our arts; but we may doubt whether the obsession with being a genius is of any value to the lesser artist. If the only race he will enter for is the Grand Genius Stakes, then we are obliged to grant some justice to the philistines' constant complaint about the selfish obscurity and technical poverty of modern art. But in any case a completely new factor is about to complicate this problem.

64 The cybernetic revolution is going to give us much more leisure; and one of the ways in which we shall have to fill that leisure must be in the practice of the arts. It is obvious that we cannot all pretend to be geniuses; and as obvious that we must give up our present contempt for the craft aspect of art.

65 It is as much craftmanship as 'genius' that will fill in the abysses and oceans of leisure in the world to come; that will educate and analyse the self; that will console it. Here and there the craftsman will border on, even become the genius. For there are no frontiers here; no one can say before the journey where the one ends and the other begins; they may be eternity apart, they may be a second—that second in which the real poet has the line, the painter the inner sight, the composer the sound; that instantaneous force that through the green fuse drives the flower.

THE STYLE IS NOT THE MAN

66 Our obsession with the idea of genius has led us into another fallacy: that the style is the man. But just as in physics we begin to realize the extent of our knowledge—what we can know and what we can never know—so in art we have reached the extremes in

techniques. We have used words in all the extreme ways, sounds in all the extreme ways, shapes and colours in all the extreme ways; all that remains is to use them within the bounds of the extreme ways already developed. We have reached the end of our field. Now we must come back, and discover other occupations than reaching the end of fields.

67 What will matter finally is intention; not instrumentation. It will be skill in expressing one's meaning with *styles*, not just in one style carefully selected and developed to signal one's individuality rather than to satisfy the requirements of the subject-matter. This is not to remove the individual from art or to turn artistic creation into a morass of pastiche; if the artist has any genuine originality it will pierce through all its disguises. The whole meaning and commitment of the person who creates will permeate his creations, however varied their outward form.

68 We see this polystylism already in two of the greatest, and certainly the two most characteristic, geniuses of our age; Picasso and Stravinsky. And if two such artists, authentic masters, have discovered new freedoms by sacrificing the nemo-induced 'security' of a single style, then surely the craft-artists of the new leisure societies may wisely follow suit.

69 We pay far too much heed to recognizability: the artist's ability to make all his work typical of his style. It pleases the would-be connoisseur in us. Now it is true that every style and technique has to be explored; and a rapid migration through style after style, as every art student knows, is not the best method of producing satisfying work. But there is a balance to be struck.

POETRY AND HUMANITY

70　I do not believe, as it is fashionable in this democratic age to believe, that the great arts are equal; though, like human beings, they have every claim to equal rights in society. Literature, in particular poetry, is the most essential and the most valuable. In what follows, by 'poetry' I mean whatever is memorably expressed in words: principally but not necessarily what is ordinarily meant by poetry.

71　The 'languages' of the other arts are all languages of the mind minus words. Music is the language of aural sensation; painting, of visual; sculpture, of plastic-visual. They are all language substitutes of one kind or another, though in certain fields and situations these language substitutes are far more effective in communicating than verbal language proper. Visual art can convey appearance better than words, but as soon as it tries to convey what lies behind visual appearance, words are increasingly likely to be of more use and value. Similarly music can convey sound, and very often generalized emotion, better than words; but with the same disadvantage when we try to go beyond the surface of the sound or the emotions it evokes.

72　The language of music can convey natural sound and can create sound which is pleasurable purely as sound; but we think chiefly of it as an evoker of emotion. It reproduces natural sounds far better than words, which have only the clumsy technique of onomatopoeia; it creates pure sound as words can only if they are largely deprived of meaning, and then only within the narrow range of the human voice. But it evokes emotion in a characteristically imprecise way, unless descriptive words (as in a programme title or a libretto) or historical convention link the emotion verbally to some precise situation.*

73 Visual art has to deal with the mask; the artist may know what lies behind the appearance of what he paints or draws or sculpts, and we say of some visual artefacts, such as good portraits, that they 'tell' us about the subject. They may do this because, as Lavater believed of all human physiognomy, the appearance happens to reveal what lies behind; but they are more likely to do so because the artist translates his verbal knowledge of what lies behind the appearance into distortions or special emphases of the mask of appearance that reveal the 'secret' behind—a process that ends in caricature.

74 This distortion process has an advantage; it allows some, perhaps most, of the 'secret' behind, of the real character behind the appearance, to be grasped at a glance. If I am adequately to explain in words the sadness of this Rembrandt self-portrait, I must study his entire work and his biography. The iconographic entry into the reality of his life takes, for any except the professional critic, only a few minutes; the verbal-biographic will take at least several hours, and perhaps much longer.

75 There is the same comparative immediacy of effect, of communication, in music; in, say, the welling sadness of the adagio from Mozart's G minor quintet. But the disadvantage of this immediacy is that, without verbal knowledge of the circumstances of Rembrandt's or Mozart's life, I have only a very imprecise knowledge of the true nature of their sadness. I know its intensity, but not its cause. I am once again faced with a mask, which may be very beautiful and

moving, but behind which I can really penetrate only with words. In short, both the visual and the aural arts sacrifice accuracy of information to speed and convenience of communication.

76 This both justifies and evaluates them. Being human is wanting to do and to know and to feel and to understand many things in a short span; and any way of making that knowing, feeling and understanding more available to the many is justifiable. But the quality of knowing and understanding, and ultimately of feeling, must be inferior in the visual and aural arts to that in poetry. All the achievements of visual art beyond direct representation of appearance are in a sense the triumphs of a deaf-mute over his deaf-muteness, just as in music the triumphs are those of a blind mute over his mute blindness.

77 The stock reply in this often-used analogy is that literature is both blind and deaf: not being mute is its specific grace. But the incontrovertible fact is that there is no artefact in the other arts that could not be more or less precisely defined by words, while there are countless artefacts and situations in literature that cannot even in the vaguest way be defined by the 'languages' of the other arts. We have neither the time nor the vocabulary nor the desire to describe the great majority of aural and visual artefacts in words, but they are all ultimately describable; and the converse is not so.

78 The word is inherent in every artistic situation, if for no other reason than that we can analyse our feelings about the other arts only in words. This is because the word is man's most precise and inclusive tool; and poetry is the using of this most precise and inclusive tool memorably.

79 Some scientists say that man's most precise tool is the mathematical symbol; semantically some equations and theorems appear to have a very austere and genuine poetry. But their precision is a precision in a special domain abstracted, for perfectly good practical reasons, from the complexity of reality. Poetry does not make this abstraction of a special domain in order to be more precise. Science is, legitimately, precision at all cost; and poetry, legitimately, inclusion at all cost.

80 *Science is always in parenthesis; poetry is not.*

81 Some technological philosophers and scientists dismiss memorable poetic statements as no more than brilliant generalizations or statements of emotional attitude, whose only significant value is as historical data or bits of biographical description of the poet. To these bigots, all statements not statistically or logically verifiable are supposedly tinsel, pretty carnival gew-gaws remote from the sobriety of the allegedly most real reality: their notion of science.

82 If he had been such a scientist, Shakespeare would have begun Hamlet's famous soliloquy with some properly applicable statement, such as 'The situation in which I find myself is one where I must carefully examine the arguments for and against suicide, never forgetting that the statements I shall make are merely emotional verbal statements about myself and my own present situation and must not be taken to constitute any statement about any other person or situation or to constitute anything more than biographical data'.

83 *Nobis cum semel occidit brevis lux, nox est perpetua una dormienda.* When once our short life has burnt

away, death is an unending sleep. This is a totally unverifiable statement, but it is a proof that other standards exist besides verifiability. Why else has it been countlessly remembered for two thousand years?

84 The 'brilliant generalizations' of great poetry are not pseudo-equations or pseudo-definitions, because the things and emotions they summarize and define exist, yet cannot be summarized or defined in any other way. The situation about which most poetic statements are made is so complex that only such a statement can make it. Just as the equation may be proved useless because of errors about the data its symbols are based on, so may the poetic statement be 'disproved' because it is not sufficiently memorable —not semantically perceptive enough or, non-semantically, not well enough expressed. The better poet disproves the worse.

85 I think of two poets whose poetry I have a special love for: Catullus and Emily Dickinson. If their poetry were not to exist, no amount of historical and biographical information about them, no amount of music or painting they might have made, no quantity even (were such a thing possible) of interviewing and meeting them, could compensate me for the loss of the precise knowledge of their deepest reality, their most real reality, that their poems give. I wish there was a head of Catullus, I wish there was more than one miserable daguerreotype of Emily Dickinson, and a recording of her voice: but these are trivial lacks beside the irreplaceability the absence of their poetries would represent.

86 Poetry is under attack from every side; it is under attack from science, more than the other arts are, because like science it deals in meaning, though

generally it is not meaning in the same situations or
with the same purposes as technological science. It is
under attack from the other arts, though this is in-
directly rather than directly; and it is under attack
from the historical situation.

87 Poetry is often despised because it is not an art with
an 'international language' like music and painting.
It pays the penalty for having the precisest tool. But
it is this tool that makes it the most open art, the
least exploitable and the least tyrannizable.

88 Many people maintain that the poets have only themselves to blame for the unhappy state their art is in.
Certainly they are guilty—and have been guilty since
the Symbolist Movement—of a dangerous confusion
between the 'language' of music and language proper.
A note has no meaning in itself, but gains whatever
meaning it has by being put in a series of other notes,
and even then, in a harmonic group or melodic series,
its meaning will vary with the temperament, race and
musical experience of the listener. Music is a 'lan-
gauge' whose chief beauty is multiple meaning, and
even then, nonlinguistic multiple meaning; in short,
music is not a language, so the metaphor is false. But
poetry uses a language which must have meaning;
most of the so-called 'musical' devices in poetry—
alliteration, euphony, assonance, rhyme—are in fact
rhythmical devices, adjuncts of metre. The true sister
of poetry is dancing, which preceded music in the
history of man. It is from this historic confusion between music and poetry that some of the uncontrolled
spread of complex imagery and ambiguity in the
postsymbolist arts has come. Mallarmé and his fol-
lowers tried to effect a shotgun marriage between
music and poetry. They tried to put the shiftingness,
the changing flow, the shimmering essence of Wag-

nerian and Debussyan music into their words, but the words could not bear the burden; and so, since the word sounds would not sufficiently shimmer, the word meanings had to. I am not belittling the courage or the beauty of Mallarmé's work; but the practical modern result in all the arts of this confusion is this: it is cleverness with symbols, ability to shift them about, to establish and dissolve patterns, to be oblique, to proceed by a semantic differential calculus when a simple addition would be enough, that is alleged to be specifically 'modern' and creatively most valid. Of course it can be modern and valid; it is the *specifically* and the *most* that we should take less for granted.*

89 Though, like all the arts, poetry condenses, selects, distorts and emphasizes in order to present its view of reality, its very precision and the enormously complicating factor of linguistic meaning make it less immediate; and in an age neurotically aware of the *brevis lux* and the night to come, it is immediacy that the audiences want. But poetry is still even now more a nation's anima, its particular mystery, its adytum, than any other of the arts.

90 If at the moment it seems less relevant it is because the sudden flood of mechanized techniques of presenting the visual and aural arts is producing a general linguistic anaemia, a debilitation of language, throughout the world. The majority, consisting largely at this stage of evolution of a recently emancipated proletariat to whom art is still much more an incidental source of pleasure than a fundamental source of truth, naturally *hear* beauty and *see* beauty more easily than they can find it in thinking, imagining and apprehending linguistic meaning.

91 This bias could be corrected in our educational systems. Most large schools have art and music teachers. A poetry teacher is at least as important; and the ability to teach the writing of poetry is *not* the same as the ability to teach the grammar and literature of the language.

92 What is even more ominous for poetry is the fact that since the Second World War a new kind of intellectual has emerged in large numbers. He is chiefly interested in art, in the cinema, in photography, in dress fashions, interior decoration and the rest. His world is bounded by colour, shape, texture, pattern, setting, movement; and he is only minimally interested in the properly intellectual (moral and socio-political) significance of events and objects. Such people are not really intellectuals, but *visuals*.

93 A visual is always more interested in style than in content, and more concerned to see than to understand. A visual does not *feel* a rioting crowd being machine-gunned by the police; he simply sees a brilliant news photograph.

94 Poets are essentially defenders of order and meaning. If they have so often in the past attacked actual human orders and meanings, it was to establish a better order and meaning. Absolute reality is chaos and anarchy, from our relative human standpoint; and our poets are our ultimate corps of defence. If we think poetry of least concern among our arts, we are like generals who disband their best fighting troops.

95 Cherish the poet; there seemed many great auks till the last one died.

11

THE ARISTOS IN THE
INDIVIDUAL

1   I hope it is now clear what kind of acceptances and
    sacrifices and changes I believe we must make to
    arrive at the Aristos, the best for our situation at this
    time. But the word *aristos* is also an adjective and
    can be applied to the individual. What can be said of
    the ideal man to achieve this best situation?

2   First and foremost we cannot expect him always to
    be the *aristos*. We are all sometimes of the Many.
    But he will avoid membership. There can be no or-
    ganization to which he fully belongs; no country, no
    class, no church, no political party. He needs no uni-
    form, no symbols; his ideas are his uniform, his ac-
    tions are his symbols, because above all he tries to be
    a free force in a world of tied forces.

3   He knows the difference between himself and the
    Many cannot be one of birth or wealth or power or
    cleverness. It can only be based on intelligent and
    enacted goodness.

4   He knows everything is relative, nothing is absolute.
    He sees one world with many situations; not one
    situation. For him, no judgement stands; and he will
    not permanently join because if he permanently
    joins with others, however intelligent, however well-
    intentioned, he helps to constitute an elect, a Few.

He knows from history that sooner or later every congregation of the elect is driven to condone bad means to good ends; then they cease to be a congregation of the elect and become a mere oligarchy.

5 He accepts the necessity of his suffering, his isolation, and his absolute death. But he does not accept that evolution cannot be controlled and its dangers limited.

6 He believes that the only human aim is contentment; and that it is the best aim because it can never be fulfilled. For progress changes, but does not reduce, the enemies of human contentment.

7 He knows the Many are not only a besieged army; but starved of equality, a seditious besieged army. They are like prisoners vainly and laboriously trying to file their way through massive iron bars in order to reach a blue sky in which they could not possibly exist; while all the time, just behind them, their cell waits to be properly lived in.

8 He knows we all live at the crossroad of myriad irreconcilable poles, or opposing factors. Their irreconcilability constitutes our cell, and the discovery of living with, and utilizing, this irreconcilability constitutes our escape.

9 He knows all religious and political creeds are *faute de mieux;* are utilities.

10 He knows the Many are like an audience under the spell of a conjuror, seemingly unable to do anything but serve as material for the conjuror's tricks; and he knows that the true destiny of man is to become a magician himself.

11 And he knows all these things because he himself is one of the Many.

12 To accept one's limited freedom, to accept one's isolation, to accept this responsibility, to learn one's particular powers, and then with them to humanize the whole: that is the best for this situation.

APPENDIX

The original impetus for these notes, and many of the ideas in them, came from Heraclitus. He was alive at Ephesus in Asia Minor five hundred years before Christ. That is certain; all the rest is more or less plausible legend. It is said that he was of a ruling family, but refused to rule; that he went to the best schools but claimed that he had educated himself; that he preferred playing with children and wandering about the mountains to listening to the glossy platitudes of his eminent contemporaries; that he was invited by Darius to his court, but refused; that he loved riddles and was called the 'Dark', that he hated the masses of his day, the Many, and that he died miserably. All that remains of his teaching can be printed in a dozen pages. The following are the main fragments of his teaching, some original and some as filtered through in the Hippocratic corpus.

*

This world, which is the same for all, was made by neither a god nor a man.

The opposite is beneficial.

If it were not for injustice, men would not know justice.

War [all biological conflict] *is justice, because everything comes into being through War.*

The beginning and the end are the same.

Even sleepers are workers.

The keraunos [the thunderbolt, chaos, hazard] *steers all things.*

Change is rest.

All that we see is death.

The one and only wisdom is both willing and unwilling to be called God.

Humanity has no understanding; but the Logos [divine law, evolution] *has.*

How can you hide from what is always present?

It is not better that men should have all they want.

Man, like a light in the night, is kindled and put out.

To God, all things are good and fair and just. It is men who suppose that some things are just, others unjust.

The Many turn their backs on what concerns them most.

The one most in repute knows what is reputed, and no more. But justice will always overtake the liars and charlatans.

Much learning does not teach understanding.

The Many know neither how to listen nor how to speak.

The Many pray to images, as if they could speak to houses. They do not understand either gods or philosophers.

Dionysus [ritualistic religion] *is the same as hell.*

The Many misinterpret the events of their lives; they learn of things; and then they think they know them.

Even asses know straw is better than gold.

Though the Logos [the law of evolution] *is ubiquitous, the Many behave as if each had a private wisdom of his own.*

Custom and nature do not agree, for the Many formed custom without understanding nature.

As a child to the man, man to the Logos.

The aristos [the good man by Heraclitus' definition of what constitutes good—independence of judgement and the pursuit of inner wisdom and inner knowledge] *is worth ten thousand others.*

Wisdom consists of one thing—to know what steers all through all.

Those who are awake [each aristos] *have one world in common, those who are asleep* [the Many] *live each in a private world.*

All men have one concern: to know themselves, and be sober.

The greatest virtue is to say and act the truth within the limitations of nature.

Sometimes obey one only.

Gold miners dig much and find little.

To verify statements and to make original statements require equal intelligence.

Nightwalkers [lovers of obscurity], *Magians* [professional mystifiers], *priests of Bacchus and priestesses of the vat, and the initiated* [the elect who brag of their election] *are evil.*

Religious rites are unholy.

Lovers of wisdom must know many things.

A dry soul is wisest and best.

Man grows from his smallest to his greatest by removing excess and remedying deficiency.

The oracle at Delphi neither hides nor states, but gives signs.

What sense have they [so-called educated men]? *They follow the names in repute and are influenced by the Many, not seeing that among the names in repute there are many bad and few good. But the aristos chooses one thing above all others—immortal glory among mortals, while the Many glut themselves like beasts.*

Man must cling to what is common to all, as a city clings to its laws.

Time is as a child playing draughts.

Dogs also bark at a man they do not know [the Many and the aristos].

If you do not expect it, you will not find out the unexpected.

The road up and the road down are the same road.

Potters use a wheel that goes neither forwards nor backwards, yet goes both ways at once. So it is like the cosmos. On this wheel is made pottery of every shape and yet no two pieces are identical, though all are made of the same materials and with the same tools.

What is not cannot come into being. From where will it come? But all diminishes and increases to the greatest possible maximum and the least possible minimum. 'Becoming' and 'perishing' are popular expressions; they are really 'mixing' and 'separating'. Becoming and perishing are the same thing, mixing and separating are the same thing; increase and diminution are the same thing; they are all the same thing and so is the relation of the individual to all things, and all things to the individual; yet in spite of appearances nothing of all things is the same.

Men saw a log, one pushes, the other pulls. But in doing this they are doing the same thing. While making less, they make more. Such is the nature of man.

Fire and water are sufficient for one another and for everything else. But each by itself is sufficient neither for itself nor for anything else. Neither can become the complete master. When fire has finished all the water, it lacks nourishment, and conversely the water with the fire. Its motion fails, it stops, what remains of the other attacks. If either were to be mastered, nothing would be as it is. Fire and water suffice for all that exists to their maximum and minimum degree alike.

NOTES

References are to page and paragraph numbers.

13.3: Many modern philosophers. The classic statement of their position was made by the Viennese Circle in the *Wissenschaftliche Weltauffassung* of 1929.

'The metaphysicians and theologians, misinterpreting their own sentences, believe that their sentences assert something, represent some state of affairs. Nevertheless, analysis shows that these sentences do not say anything, being instead only an expression of some emotional attitude. To express this may certainly be a significant task. However, the adequate means for its expression is art, for example lyric poetry or music.'

16.15: Pangloss. The pedantic old tutor to the hero in Voltaire's *Candide* (1759). His incurable and misleading optimism brought him nothing but misfortune.

17.19: supernovae. A supernova is a star that explodes as a result of violent internal changes of pressure, which lead to an equally violent nuclear reaction. In the first *second* of such an explosion as much energy may be released as in the course of *1,000 million years* of the star's normal nuclear reaction processes. Such explosions may have an intense phase of a fortnight or more, and all life on the supernova's own and neighbouring stars' planetary systems would be charred to nothingness. Professor Fred Hoyle has calculated that *in our own galaxy alone* there are at least 100,000 million stars capable of evolving human life on their planetary systems.

20.35: Emily Dickinson. The great and lonely American poetess (1830–1886) whose brilliant command of paradox was married to a profound insight into the nature of human suffering. The line quoted is the central theme of much of her work: if life were one long happy summer, we should be without the mysterious truths we learn from our 'winters' of suffering.

21.42: A phoenix infinity. The mythical bird phoenix, supposed to be the only one of its kind and to live for five or six hundred years, lit its own funeral pyre and then sprang reborn and young again from its own ashes. The red shift referred to in the previous paragraph is the proof—from spectographic analysis—that very distant objects in our universe are receding from us; a blue shift would indicate that they are falling back on us, and that a universal holocaust was one day inevitable.

22.51: St. Augustine. Bishop of Hippo, and author of *The Confessions.*

23.54: Tao Te Ching: Exceedingly difficult to translate, but roughly 'The Classic concerning the System that governs all and the Nature of things'. It was formerly ascribed to Lao Tzu ('Old Man'), a supposed contemporary of Confucius (551–479 BC). Modern scholars now believe that Lao Tzu was the name of the book, not of the author; and that it is really an anthology of Taoist thought from the fourth and third centuries before Christ, designed primarily to give advice to the wise as to how to live through the troubled times of the Warring States period (480–222 BC). Politically and socially it recommends meekness and submission—the art of survival at all costs. But what makes it one of the great monuments of human thought is its attempt to describe the indescribable—the nature of God and of human existence. The Tao (way or system or divine principle) is often described as *wu wei* and *wu ming*—without action (in human affairs) and without name (indescribable in words). There are some strange parallels with pre-Socratic Greek thought.

26.62: contingent. Used here, of course, in the sense of 'conditional' or 'non-essential'.

27.71: Erigena. Otherwise known as Johannes Scotus (c. 815–877). Philosopher and theologian.

29.4: The Bet Situation. From the famous *pensée* of Pascal. *Il faut parier. Cela n'est pas volontaire: vous êtes embarqué.* (You must bet. You have no choice: you are in the game.)

45.71: stasis. Stoppage of the circulation of the blood.

52.23: My contention here was tragically borne out by the Robert Kennedy assassination. At the preliminary hearing, Sirhan's greatest concern was that his name should be correctly spelt and pronounced. There is something almost parasitical in such acts: now Sirhan's name will be remembered as long as Bobby Kennedy's.

74.29: amour courtois. The code of 'knightly love' that dominated educated Europe in the early Middle Ages had as its central principle the idea that truly noble love is never consummated. It was, so to speak, a game without a prize—and whose only purpose could therefore be the continuance of the game.

102.2: Ernst Mach. Austrian physicist and psychologist (1836–1916).

104.9: Kierkegaardian step in the dark. The argument of the Danish philosopher is that at some point in all the major decisions of life (for Kierkegaard, of course, the greatest was whether or not to be a Christian) reason and intelligence and scholarship become powerless to help; so one must either live in perpetual doubt and anguish or step into the dark.

Tertullian. Tertullian (c. 155–222) came, like Saint Augustine, from near Carthage. He too led a wicked youth, turned to Christianity in his later years, and became the greatest theologian and apologist of his time. His most famous statement of position is his *credibile quia ineptum*—it is credible because it is absurd.

114.43: Odi profanum . . . 'I loathe the vulgar crowd, and shun them'—from Horace. He was given the Sabine farm —which remains a delicious rural retreat only twenty miles from Rome—by the millionaire Maecenas.

115.47: the ancient Milesians. The pre-Socratic philosophers. Miletus ought to be ranked with Athens, Rome and Paris for its importance in the growth of the European spirit.

Orphic mysticism. The associated cults of Orpheus and Dionysus—both gods of the senses—relied on music, alcohol and ritual to gain and hold adherents. These cults probably had much in common with more recent African secret-society 'religions'. Apollo stands for reason, law, moderation.

130.27: 'feelies'. From *Brave New World*—movies that can be felt as well as seen and heard.

152.40: an artefact. Artefact properly means any artificial object (as opposed to natural object), but since 'works of art' has come to be applied to painting and sculpture only, I use *artefact* here in the sense of any creation of man in any of the arts.

158.65: Laius and Jocasta. The parents of Oedipus.

171.112: Meaulnes. From *Le Grand Meaulnes,* by Alain-Fournier. One of the great parables of that aspect of the European spirit that prefers the dream to the reality. *Domaine perdu, domaine sans nom:* lost place, place without a name.

172.116: nostalgie de la vierge. Nostalgia for the girl. Nabokov's Lolita was symptomatic of a general twentieth century tendency, and one that is reciprocated by a nostalgia for the father in girls. Though physical virginity has lost its attraction for men, the chief drive in these girl–father relationships seems to be the mutual attraction of inexperience and experience; and this is reinforced by the typical consumer-society belief that the latest model is the best. The consumer's pleasure is what counts; unfortunately in this case the discarded model is another human being.

176.124: persona. The literal meaning is 'mask', as used by actors in the Greek and Roman theatre.

181.142: Adler. Alfred Adler (1870–1937), the Austrian psychologist, believed that Freud overemphasized the sexual motives of human behaviour. Adler considered much more attention should be paid to the individual's striving for superiority and power over others.
  Karen Horney. A German woman psychologist (1885–1952) who was greatly influenced both by Adler and by her experience of the United States, where she lived for the last twenty years of her life. She placed stress on the need for security as a fundamental psychological drive, and believed that much neurosis was caused by environment rather than by disturbance in childhood.

184.3: noösphere. A term coined by Teilhard de Chardin, the French Jesuit philosopher and anthropologist who died in 1955. In the noösphere there is no time—but only the placeless and ageless thoughts and creations of the human spirit in art and science, which encircle our present lives as the atmosphere encircles the earth.

196.41: aleatory. The term (from the Latin *alea,* a dice-game) used to describe all those modern creative techniques that rely on hazard.

198.52: lycanthropism. Literally, the desire to be a were-wolf, but used of those forms of schizophrenic madness in which the patient has phases in which he imagines himself to be some beast and exhibits depraved appetites —the Jekyll-and-Hyde personality.

204.72: onomatopoeia. The formation of words that sound like what they describe—hiss, bang, murmur, etc.

209.88: Mallarmé. Stephane Mallarmé (1842–98), the greatest poet of the Symbolist school, whose most famous work is *L'Après-midi d'un Faune,* on which Debussy based his piece. The Symbolists erected metonymy, the literary device of suggesting instead of directly stating what one means, as the chief mode of poetic expression. One of Mallarmé's best-known sonnets begins: *Is the fresh, vivacious and beautiful today going to break with a drunken blow of the wing that stern forgotten lake which the transparent glacier of flights that have not flown haunts beneath the frost?* These lines are generally taken to refer to the agonizing difficulty Mallarmé sometimes had in composing his poems; but other meanings are possible. It is this deliberate ambiguity of meaning that has dominated all modern art since Mallarmé.